CONVERSION

CONVERSION

A. J. Krailsheimer

SCM PRESS LTD

334 01950 8

First published 1980
by SCM Press Ltd
58 Bloomsbury Street, London WC1

Typeset by Input Typesetting Ltd, London
and printed in Great Britain by
Billing & Sons Ltd,
Guildford, London and Worcester

Contents

Introduction

Christianity is not the only world religion in which conversion experiences occur, nor indeed are such experiences confined to religion in its strict sense; secular creeds, like Marxism or Maoism, have their converts too. There does, however, seem to be in the various forms of Christianity one essential feature which is not to be found even in its closest analogues, Judaism and Islam. The truth of Christianity as proclaimed from the time of Christ throughout the ages is that the Christian enters into a special, personal relationship with God through Christ. The call 'forsake all and follow me' can be paralleled in most, possibly all, master-disciple religions, but the idea of answering the call in terms of a strictly personal relationship with a master who is himself God and man seems to be unique to Christianity.

It must at once be said that as soon as any religion becomes established, it may live on as much through inertia as through impetus, so that the term 'believer' applied to most adherents of most world religions at most times is little more than a formal description of conformism in externals accompanied by passive acceptance of the formulas, rather than the active spiritual content, of doctrine. It is precisely because the discrepancy between practice and inner life is frequently so wide, that the phenomenon of conversion is at least as common within a Christian context as from outside into Christianity. It follows that a dramatic change in external behaviour is not the principal, or even necessary, result of conversion, but on the contrary a new relationship with Christ, however expressed, is the very definition of Christian conversion. The degree to which individual Christians, or particular groups, feel and reflect this relationship must vary enormously, and no useful purpose would be served by attempting to define even a statistical average. What seems incontrovertible is that no person or group of persons can fail to be aware, either in themselves or others, that a vital change has taken place once this relationship with Christ becomes an experienced reality instead of a pious phrase.

This is at once the domain of theology and of direct emotion, and the two are not always congenial partners. Theology is, after all, an intellectual activity, an academic discipline, alien to simple souls, too often distrustful, sometimes destructive of emotion. Emotion, on the other hand, is too often a will-o'the wisp, beckoning the unwary fatally far into the quagmire of subjectivity and self-delusion. Intellectual conviction may follow or precede conversion; it never seems to effect it alone. *Fides quaerens intellectum* (faith seeking understanding) remains the Christian norm. It is quite possible that psychology may one day order and explain the emotions involved in religious faith, but to the extent that psychology, like theology, is an intellectual activity, and now a recognized academic discipline, it is still speculative, because dependent on its non-intellectual, disordered raw material of human behaviour. This is another way of saying that conversion or relationship with Christ can quite legitimately be discussed and analysed by theologians and psychologists, but their findings will no more account for the experienced reality than a chemist analysing the difference in taste between a good and a poor wine, or an acoustics engineer trying to distinguish the aesthetic effect of a Mozart symphony from that of its 'pop' arrangement. It is to analogies of human experience that one must go for an understanding of these mysteries of faith. It is, of course, from just these analogies that Christ himself taught his first disciples, and whatever analytical techniques may later prove helpful, the basis of understanding remains the actual experience, or potential for experience, of each one of us.

At the heart of Christianity, symbol and reality in one, stands the cross: Christ dying for men. The power and glory of the creator, his mercy and justice, his goodness and truth, are familiar elements in many religions, including Christianity. Men have led, and continue to lead, better lives inspired by just such a view of God. Sometimes, notably in Judaism and Islam, the voice of such a God has come upon prophets; sometimes, as in Eastern religions, the contact has been mystical rather than verbal. In Christianity alone has it from the first moment been human and personal.

Whatever the Old Testament Jews or their successors understood or understand by their expected Messiah, Christians necessarily and invariably see Christ as saviour: specifically one who saves man from the consequence of his sin. The theological interpretation of the doctrine of original sin is far from being unanimous, but in a way this hardly matters. The men and women whose sins Christ forgave in the New Testament were not concerned with anyone's sins but their own. Whatever cause individuals may assign to their sins, be it heredity, madness or natural perversity, the guilt is theirs, and it is they who feel the need for forgiveness. The theology of redemption and atonement is again by no means unanimous, but there must be a sense in which Christians feel that Christ paid once and for all for human sins. The cross was not for someone else, it was not for the obscure sin of our remote forebears; if we feel it to mean anything, it is in relation to our personal guilt, which may, of course, be an acknowledgment of our share of collective guilt. 'Repent, for the kingdom of heaven is at hand' is a collective call, not an invitation addressed only to those whose transgressions are of a certain quantity or quality. The righteous, whoever they may be, are not called to repent, but 'in thy sight shall no man living be justified'; so it has often been the most devout and morally blameless in the eyes of others who have felt most keenly their own guilt and unworthiness.

Talk of sin and guilt inevitably conjures up images of crime and punishment, and far too much Christian literature has dwelt with relish on those aspects of the question. Like the Jews of the Old Testament, living by the Law and familiar with the penalties exacted for particular infractions, most religious and secular authorities have at all times promulgated such disciplinary measures. For centuries judicial analogies were made in art and literature between human judges and the Last Judgment, between heaven and hell and earthly rewards and punishments. However distorted and crude such analogies may be, they undoubtedly affected the attitudes of the great majority of Christians. Even those who were so affected did not stop at that. If Christians have ever seen their religion as one in which a harsh judge has to be placated, or in which one's record of vice or virtue alone determines one's fate – and this has certainly been so from time to time – it is through an aberration of human origin, owing nothing to gospel teaching as a whole but only to a few texts taken out of context. The most fearful Christians have always found a sure refuge from such terrors in God's love revealed in Christ.

Whatever some modern scholars may say, it is not possible to profess Christianity without believing in the incarnation. It is not possible to believe in the incarnation without linking the man Jesus on the cross with God's will for our redemption. And that redemption, whether seen mainly in penal terms or in terms free of penal overtones, involves love. The cross, as a historical fact,

God's love through Christ, as an eternal truth, the incarnation as the mystery linking both, these are the irreducible minima of Christian belief. In these basic tenets the personal relationship with Christ may involve service or sacrifice from us, but always and only validated by love, not fear. It is therefore more helpful to see the successive stages before and after conversion in affective rather than penal or sacrificial terms. Estrangement and alienation, reconciliation and union, are what we should be thinking about, and again, as in any human relationship, guilt and hurt, joy and understanding find their place in the spiritual chronicle.

It is notorious that to fall violently in love with another person is no guarantee of a durable relationship, frequently indeed the reverse. Similarly, arranged matches are by no means always loveless. However a relationship may begin, its value can only properly be assessed in the long term, or under stress. In all human relationships, even in those free from sexual passions like parent-children relationships, there are two parties responsible, often in very unequal degree, for their maintenance and development. This is where the analogy between even the best human relationship and that of the believer with Christ is misleading enough to break down. The notion of God's wrath has always been a powerful ingredient in Christianity, as in many other religions, but even to talk of Christ's wrath is impossible. He has already and for ever suffered patiently for every sin and slight of which human beings are capable. It is we who cut ourselves off from him, not he who rejects us. The call of Christianity is to accept his love by responding to it. The response may be sudden or gradual, his offer remains constant.

Certain steps may be taken by way of initiation (baptism or communion, for example), or equally by way of publicly professed commitment, but just as a wedding ceremony is only the public proclamation of a private relationship between two people, sanctified and recognized but in no way guaranteed against collapse, so the response to Christ's love has to be lived out, not identified with a single act or occasion, however momentous. Christian churches with a sacramental tradition offer their members a continuous cycle of renewal in the emotional and spiritual concentration of the eucharist, confession and so on; others may make preaching, or other public witness to the Word, the focal point. All recognize that the individual's prayer life needs to be constantly nourished and animated if God's love through Christ and our response to it are to be maintained as the basis of the relationship in faith. In practice being, or becoming, a Christian has always meant belonging to a community, or church, and even today when such formal allegiance is sometimes rejected by people who feel themselves to be Christian, their acts of worship will never be exclusively solitary, especially at such times as Christmas and Easter, when they will join other worshippers, perhaps on radio or television, but in some sense corporately. An inseparable part of the Christian call is to share with others the brotherhood of Christ. Even the hermit does not attempt to keep it to himself, and can indeed only survive if his prayers and meditations acknowledge the humanity whose members he may never physically encounter. A Christian solipsist is a contradiction in terms, and it would be equally absurd to imagine one Christian being jealous of God's love for another.

If most people would accept that a human relationship of a quite unique kind is a good analogy for Christianity, no one type of relationship is preeminently normative. For many woman, like St Teresa, the imagery of sexual love has conveyed the intensity and immediacy of their feelings about Christ without in any way setting these within the constraints of human sexuality. Men may think of Christ as a companion or brotherly figure; all in some sense see in him the beloved master. All that can safely be said is that any full, secure and generous relationship founded on love, but independent of passion, seems to express something of the place of Christ in the lives of individuals according to their varying affective needs and capacity. 'Now ye are children and not servants' is how he described the relationship of the disciples to his and their father, and such remains the Christian paradigm. A Christian cannot escape being a member of a family, most of whose members he will never know, and sharing with them the same rights and duties.

Implicit in the idea of conversion is that of forsaking the past unconditionally and accepting in its place a future of which the one certain fact is that it will never allow the previous pattern of life to be the same again. Everyone can understand what a notorious sinner has done if he suddenly turns into a good citizen, though it may not be apparent why the change has taken place. Socially reprehensible behaviour, ranging from the luridly criminal to the meanly nasty, is clearly a good thing to put behind one. What is not at all easy to understand is the renunciation of a respectable, useful, even admirable life of moderate, not excessive, comfort in favour of one of poverty, hardship, perhaps ignominy, and yet both changes are forms of true conversion. So too is the sudden change of spiritual, though not external, direction of monk or nun, priest or layman, who goes on performing exactly the same acts as before but for totally different reasons. In each case there has been a break, without which the entry upon a new, full spiritual life could never have been effected. One result of conversion seems always to be that the past, however apparently blameless before, begins to be revalued, even rewritten. The convert will see his newly found identity and response to Christ as real; all that previously kept him from it as shadowy, false or empty. The sense of guilt is a natural enough concomitant of a conventionally sinful life, but the sense of emptiness, 'vanity' in scriptural terms, is more fundamental. As the new relationship with Christ develops, the earlier time spent without it appears more and more of a waste.

A distinction must be made here between those who hear of Christ for the first time and those who have heard often and long enough but, perhaps unwittingly, have not heeded. In the early days of Christianity literally every Christian was a convert, and in different parts of the world at different times, right up to our own day in remote places, missionaries have brought Christianity where it had never previously been known, and there too every new Christian is a convert. In that marvellous product of the early crusading spirit, the eleventh-century *Chanson de Roland*, a neat distinction is made between the generality of the defeated Saracens at Saragossa, given an hour or two to choose between accepting Christianity and dying in various painful ways, and the Saracen queen, taken back to Charlemagne's capital, Aix, for a concentrated course of instruction, lasting several months, from suitably qualified divines, at the end of which she is solemnly baptized, and indeed takes the veil. Throughout history, and in every part of the world, conversion has been taken to include these two extremes and everything in between.

It would be fascinating and instructive to study the spiritual significance and content of such conversions throughout the ages, and the impressive number of those who have paid with hideous martyrdom for their new faith leaves no room for doubt as to its authenticity. Unfortunately the very reasons which made such men and women candidates for conversion in the first place almost always constitute practical obstacles to an objective study of their cases. Remoteness in time, in place, in linguistic expression, lack of education and literacy, witnesses who are rarely disinterested, all these factors make it hard for reliable records to exist or survive. Hagiography and missionary chronicles may be written in complete good faith, but leave too many vital questions unanswered. It is solely on that account, that is, the inadequate nature of the records, that examples from this vast and inspiring company of converts have not been included in this book. There is no reason to suppose that spiritually or psychologically they differ in any important respect from those of similar status and education whose cases are later examined here, simply because their record is full and articulate. It goes without saying that missionary converts and martyrs have rejected their old way of life, since it is normally their refusal to resume it that brings about their death. It also goes without saying that mass conversions are of necessity superficial, and to that extent unstable, and that converts relapse for the same human reasons as those for which people brought up as Christians lapse. All in all it does not seem very likely that different kinds of convert view their past in an essentially different way once they have fully embraced Christianity, but the process by which they arrive at that stage is evidently capable of wide variation.

There is another large class of people who are properly called converts, but are not discussed in these pages: those who pass from one Christian denomination to another without a radical change in their attitude to the central truths of Christianity. Leaving aside those who were coerced into change, for example by Reformation or Counter-Reformation, it does not seem that those Anglicans in the nineteenth century who, like Newman, went over to Rome, were moved so much by a new apprehension of what Christ meant for them as by the realization that their existing obedience was no longer compatible with theological convictions concerning the nature of the church, and, of course, spiritual feelings of the same kind. This is not to question the new intensity of faith and serenity of spirit they found, in that sense a true conversion, but simply to assert that their fundamental relationship to Christ demanded a new context while remaining itself unchanged. This would not be true of those many individuals who have exchanged the respectable conformism of their inherited allegiance for another, be it Roman, Anglican or Nonconformist, as the result of what they felt to be a direct call to a live faith (where previously it had been passive) associated with membership of the particular body through which the revelation came. Whenever a dead faith comes alive, in whatever formal context, the case qualifies for consideration as conversion in the terms of this enquiry.

Catholic writers on conversion have logically enough considered only conversions to Catholicism as being true, but this begs the question of what actually happens to the convert. It may well be that different churches show different patterns of conversion, and one of the objects of this book is to seek to establish patterns, but it is surely a fault of method to claim in advance that any particular church or churches has the monopoly of true Christians, that Christ manifests himself only to those professing certain views on the nature of the church. To be different is not necessarily to be better or worse, though, of course, that assertion in itself would be seen by many to be begging a very big question. At all events both Catholics and non-Catholics figure in the following pages.

The conditions demanded of those whose cases are discussed here are deliberately as rigorous as possible. Each one believed to the end of his or her life that a quite specific experience, identifiable in time and place, changed that life totally, giving sense and meaning where before there had been emptiness and confusion. In each case a first-hand account of that experience and its consequences exists, or existed, and in the absence of such an account, several otherwise attractive candidates have regretfully been passed over. Each one of those discussed was recognized as exceptional by contemporaries, and has continued after death to exercise influence by writings, or example, or both. These are by any standards quite remarkable people, and it seems far better to limit the enquiry to incontrovertibly major figures than to extend it to lesser ones or launch into generalizations only thinly supported by evidence. Since the principle of selection has been largely determined by the survival of evidence, there can be no neat symmetry of period, country, church or sex, but what there is extends over a wider spectrum than at first appeared likely. If there seems to be glaring omissions, this is almost certainly due to ignorance or defective judgment on my part, not to any desire to prove a particular thesis by suppressing inconvenient evidence. In particular my failure to include any representatives of Eastern Orthodoxy, of whom there must be many obvious candidates, reflects my linguistic and historical incapacity to deal at all adequately with the evidence.

Some omissions can be explained by the desire to achieve as much variety as possible within the inevitable limitations of space and thus to avoid undue emphasis on any one aspect. Both Claudel and Maritain are famous and distinguished converts, but the other four French candidates seemed more absolute. In the English Protestant tradition the Quaker George Fox and John Wesley gave way to Bunyan and Booth, because Fox tells us too little of his undoubtedly authentic conversion experience to be informative and Wesley came out as a less interesting person. John Donne at first looked like a candidate, but expert opinion of the chronology and interpretation of the crucial works is so divergent as to discourage any amateur speculation. No book on so vast a subject can be exhaustive, comprehensive or even fully representative, and I can ultimately justify my selection only on personal grounds; I wanted to learn more about some people than others. Every reader is bound to think of other names for inclusion.

I did not write this book as an anthology, still less as a demonstration. I wanted to reach a fuller understanding of a fundamental spiritual experience by examining in some detail the cases of a dozen exceptional men and women apparently linked by something to which they all gave the same name. Some I already knew, some I had previously overlooked, one or two I had actually disliked, but as a result of this inquiry I now feel the deepest respect for all. They have enormously enriched my understanding of conversion and of Christianity, and my hope is that others will be led by reading the stories so briefly related here to pursue their own inquiry.

1

THE MODELS:
PAUL, AUGUSTINE AND FRANCIS

All the following chapters are in chronological order, but these first three converts are combined in a single chapter to distinguish them from the others. In the first place the evidence about their lives is, in the case of Paul and Francis, much less adequately documented than those who come later, and in Augustine's case, though ample, is in some important respects obscured by cultural differences. Then each of them is of such commanding stature in Christian history that they have always been seen as models rather than illustrations. Finally, with the advent of printing, Reformation, Counter-Reformation and humanism the period around 1500 marks the beginning of an age of which our own is still recognizably the heir, as it is not of the first fifteen hundred years of the Christian era. Paul, Augustine and Francis do not stand here, as the others do, as representatives of their respective times, though they are that as well, but because no account of Christian conversion could possibly leave them out.

From the very beginning, Christianity was a faith rooted in experience. Neither intellectual system nor code of rules, the truth of Christianity involved a statement of verifiable facts about the life, death and teaching of an identifiable person together with another statement about the experiences which a growing number of other identifiable persons associated directly with those facts. To the extent that the associated experiences relate to actual phenomena in the lives of those concerned, they are certain, but both the nature of these experiences and their causality remain to this day unproven and unprovable by natural means. The earliest history of the church is inescapably relevant to all that has followed. Though nearly two thousand years later Christianity must often seem, especially to outsiders, to concentrate on intellectual systems and moral rules, though these are the probably inevitable consequences of institutionalizing any religion, the spiritual truth without which the church would be no more than a pious club and Christianity a combination of legend, ethics and metaphysics remains exactly the same.

The way in which Christians have for centuries learned about their religion and taught it to others is neatly represented by the order of the books of the New Testament: first the Gospels, then the Acts of the Apostles, then St Paul's epistles, then the other epistles, lastly Revelation. However, this is not the order in which those documents were composed, nor, it seems, does it correspond with the order in which very many of the first-century converts heard and assented to the truths of Christianity. New Testament scholarship is a minefield into which the layman ventures at his peril, but the essential facts are hardly in dispute, despite the incessant controversy as to what conclusions can be drawn from them. For present purposes, the crucial question concerns Paul's conversion, as it is related in different passages of the New Testament, and the effect this experience had on the early and subsequent development of Christianity.

Saul, as he was originally known, was born at Tarsus in Cilicia, but probably came to Jerusalem with his parents while still young. Luke speaks of him being brought up in Jerusalem, sitting at the feet of Gamaliel, an authority on the Torah, the Jewish Law, and of being a member of the strict sect known as Pharisees. Since neither Luke nor Paul himself ever refers to any occasion on which Paul actually saw Jesus, it is generally agreed that he did not even know what Jesus looked like and certainly never met him. Not long, perhaps weeks rather than months, after Jesus' death, Saul is reported by Luke as being present at the execution by stoning of Stephen, the first recorded Christian martyr, and presumably at Stephen's trial before the High Priest and his colleagues, when Stephen spoke of the significance of the death of Jesus, 'the just one', at their hands (Acts 7). Outraged like his fellow Pharisees at what seemed to them plain blasphemy, Saul took a leading part in hunting out adherents of this sect that made a mock of Jewish orthodoxy, and we know from his own later admission that many 'saints' suffered imprisonment, interrogation and death as a result of his police action. Anxious, according to

Luke, to stop the Christian rot from spreading in major centres of Jewish settlement outside Jerusalem, Saul went with a special mandate to continue the heresy hunt in Damascus and send all suspects back to Jerusalem to be dealt with. Some critics claim that he never had such a mandate and was in fact resident in Damascus rather than Jerusalem, but all agree that he was a notorious persecutor. On the road to Damascus or nearby Saul experienced a literally blinding revelation as a result of which he joined the very sect he had so savagely persecuted and in due course became its most influential exponent.

Exactly what happened we shall never know, but the details of the three accounts given in Acts (9;22;26), corroborated by various statements in Paul's epistles, provide the verbal and imaginative pattern which ever since has typified sudden and complete conversion. All the accounts in Acts, written after Paul's death and up to fifty years after the event, agree that about noon a bright light appeared, Saul fell to the ground and heard a voice asking, 'Saul, why persecutest thou me?' and in answer to his question was told 'I am Jesus whom thou persecutest.' Two of the versions add the Greek saying, 'it is hard for thee to kick against the pricks'. He is then said to have been temporarily blinded, so that he had to be led into the city. There he was visited by a Christian named Ananias, instructed to that end by God, and despite his hostile record was almost at once accepted among the community he had set out to persecute. Whether Luke invented or arranged the actual details is immaterial for the subsequent influence they had. We know from Paul that he had a sudden conversion, and ever since Acts was written Luke's account has been accepted and repeated without question.

Paul, to give him the more familiar Greek name by which he is known as an apostle, at once began preaching his new faith in and around Damascus and was soon as much anathema to his former orthodox brethren as he had been up till then to the Christians. The long record of punishments received and dangers borne began to take shape, and in the epistles written some twenty years later, he speaks as though the transition from persecutor to persecuted had been virtually instantaneous. An important element in the story of Paul is the way in which his credentials were accepted at Damascus, and the fact that it was more than two years before he made the not very long journey to Jerusalem, where in the course of a stay lasting only two weeks he at last met Peter and James, but apparently no other Christian leaders. Peter, too, accepted his credentials, and when Paul set out on his first missionary journey (usually dated *c*.46, but perhaps as early as 37) he clearly did so with full apostolic authority. After an interval variously explained, he went back to Jerusalem (*c*.49) for a second and, in his own view, far more important visit when most of the Christian leaders gathered in what is sometimes called the 'Council of Jerusalem' to resolve major points of policy.

The chronology is not too clear, but it seems most likely that fully fourteen years elapsed between the two visits to Jerusalem (or possibly between his conversion and the second visit) and that he spent some or all of this period in Syria and his native Cilicia, or, also possible, accomplishing the greater part of his ministry in the Eastern Mediterranean. In other words, the point underlined by Paul in the Epistle to the Galatians containing this information is that during that time he was giving, not receiving, instruction in the faith. When he was executed in Rome (*c*. 67) he left as the oldest surviving documents of the Christian faith that portion (surely small) of his total correspondence known to us as his epistles, antedating all four Gospels as well as Luke's account of Paul's ministry in Acts. The preponderant influence that those few letters have exercised on Christianity ever since underlines once more the question of his credentials.

It must be said straight away that such personal qualities as intimate knowledge of Jewish teaching, ability to preach and write convincingly in several languages, to inspire and organize others, all these things were seen as quite secondary to the fact that he claimed, and was believed by all, to have *seen* the risen Christ in a special sense applied to no other persons after the ascension. That alone constituted the basis of his acceptance by the first Christians and his authority to expound the faith to Jew and Gentile alike.

Two comparisons help to make the point. In the verses of Acts 8 immediately preceding the first mention of Saul/Paul and his conversion comes an account of the conversion by Philip of the Ethiopian eunuch (a high court official). Philip had been, with Stephen, among the seven appointed by the original twelve disciples (after Judas' replacement) for a special ministry, often called that of deacon. He may well have listened to Christ teaching, seen him die, been present when he appeared to his followers after Easter, in whatever way that experience may be interpreted. His authority was that of one directly commissioned by Christ's closest collaborators, supplementing his own knowledge of Christ from eye-witness accounts. When Philip met the Ethiopian in the desert, driving home in his chariot, the man was reading the book of Isaiah, which, at his invitation, Philip interpreted in terms of Christ's life, teaching and resurrection, to such effect that the Ethiopian broke his journey to ask for immediate baptism. Such authority, transmitted directly through the disciples and those appointed by them throughout the ages, has been one of the norms in the Church, and such conversions go with that authority.

The example of Peter is even more striking. Chosen by Christ himself to be among his original followers, a commanding personality in his own right, and treated by Christ as an obvious favourite, perhaps (depending on complex arguments about the text) designated by Christ to lead the church after his death, his authority as a friend and eye-witness of Christ was unrivalled. Yet Paul waited more than two years to meet him and win his approval, later argued bitterly with him over an incident in Antioch involving a fundamental principle (the respective rights as Christians of Jews and Gentiles) and won, and from first to last neither deferred to Peter's personal authority nor, more importantly, sustained any successful challenge to his own authority from Peter and his supporters.

The reason for Paul's initial acceptance and subsequent authority up to our own day is the same rock on which all Christianity is founded: not eye-witness accounts of Christ's brief ministry nor verbatim reports of his teaching, but the attested fact of his death and resurrection, together with a résumé of the spiritual, rather than the verbal, content of the teaching. From the earliest times the ritual meal of fellowship modelled on the Last Supper formed a regular, weekly proof of mutual recognition and sharing in Christ. Thus the actual events in which Christ had taken part remained the indispensable historical basis without which no point of departure would have been possible, but instead of the fading memory of the generation that had known him, and later repetition of their story, his lasting presence as revealed in countless ways by the Spirit became the foundation of continuing faith.

In a famous passage (I Corinthians 15.8) Paul recounts the recorded appearances of the risen Christ, concluding with the last, to himself, 'least of the apostles, not meet to be called an apostle'. It is remarkable that this affirmation and the experience it denotes should have enabled Paul in his turn to bring so many Jews and Gentiles to acknowledge faith in Christ. Those who had walked with Christ in his life and could repeat his words from their own recollection had no greater authority, made no greater number of converts than Paul, the new recruit.

Thus from the very first the possibility of a direct experience of the risen Lord was an integral part of the gospel preached to those who had never heard of Christ, and knew nothing of Jewish scripture. Where such a possibility is recognized, a model and even an expectation are created. It cannot have been long before the historical memories of Christ's earthly life had receded so far into an irretrievable past that it became more important to meditate on how he revealed himself to men after Easter (or Ascension). Such revelation was open to all, recreated in a sense at each sharing of the eucharist and re-enacted each time a new convert saw the light. The fact that Paul's revelation had been without parallel, and was to remain so, cannot have been as clear in the first century as it is to-day.

Paul's experience on the road to Damascus is part of the Christian heritage, no less than Christ's acceptance of publicans and sinners, people like Mary Magdalen and social outcasts like the Samaritan woman. The difference is that before his conversion Paul had led a moral and devout life according to the Law. When he turned his back on the past it was not simply, or mainly, against the persecution he had so ruthlessly conducted, but against the cause in the name of which he had acted, the Law. So much was this the case that in Paul the antithesis is stark between the bondage of the Law and the freedom of grace. Sinners do not love their sin, and are certainly not respected for it, so their conversion effectively frees them from bonds they recognize. Paul's conversion, on the other hand, tore him away from what he and his most respected fellow Jews loved most fervently, that very righteousness spelled out in detail in scripture, that attachment to divine service and good works which every devout Jew practised in order to win God's favour. For Paul to embrace the cause of one who died a felon's death on the shameful cross (a cursed end in the eyes of pious Jews) was a reversal of values far more dramatic than for a social outcast to cling to the previously unheard promise of rehabilitation and self-respect. The source of Paul's pride was suddenly transformed into a source of shame; as he put it, he could find glory only in Christ. No wonder that Gentiles listened to this Jew who offered full membership of this new brotherhood without even the burdensome obligation of circumcision, dietary laws or Sabbath keeping. A God, a truth that could change men so radically could not be ignored.

It is wholly to Paul's credit that he never disowned his Jewish origins; never sought, even with Gentiles, to minimize the value of the Old Testament as a record of God's ways to man and a prophecy of the saviour to come; and indeed saw Christianity as the authentic continuation of Judaism. All Paul's resistance to Christianity had come from scrupulous regard for the letter of the Law, and his conversion marked the final collapse of this resistance. In so far as he felt guilt it was for the pride which had made him believe that his good deeds and moral virtue could earn him, as of right, what he later realized could only come as a gift from God through Christ. In the language of later theology, his earlier reliance on works was replaced by faith alone, which in turn inspired works.

In the two and a half centuries which elapsed between Paul's execution in Rome and Constantine's Edict of Milan (*c.* 313), recognizing the rights of the Christian church, the pattern of growth included conversion, persecution and, regrettably, doctrinal controversy. The sheer size and spread of the church militated against the intimacy of apostolic times, and dissension could only be dealt with, if at all, by trying to impose authority, often at the cost of schism, usually after protracted debate. Not long after the Edict of Milan, St Augustine was born. Probably the most influential, certainly one of the most controversial of Church Fathers, Augustine also occupies a quite special place in the history of conversion through the remarkable account he has left of his own in his *Confessions*. In excellence of literary form and interest of content this spiritual autobiography would have attracted a wide readership even if its author had not been one of the foremost theologians in the history of the church. As it is, the account of Augustine's conversion remains a literary and spiritual model of its kind to this day. Much more circumstantial than Paul, Augustine may properly be ranked next among Christian converts both in time and in importance.

Modern scholarship makes it possible to go beyond the account given in the *Confessions* and reconstruct a more historically accurate picture of Augustine's evolution. As with Paul, however, it is not the historical facts (known, after all, to very few at the time) but the version presented in an authoritative text that has proved influential. Augustine was born in 354 at Thagaste in Numidia (now Souk Ahras in Northern Algeria) of a devoutly Christian mother, Monica, and a father Patricius, baptized only late in life, who does not seem to have had much influence over his son. Shortly before his father died (372) Augustine went to Carthage, the most important city of the province, and took a concubine, who gave him a son, Adeodatus, probably in 373. There was nothing either unusual or scandalous in the liaison, and many young Christians of Augustine's social class lived in what would now be called a common-law marriage with a social inferior until the complicated arrangements for a financially advantageous match with some girl of their own class could be made. All the same, such precocious paternity must have made its mark on an emotional development which was critically important for Augustine's subsequent spiritual development.

The sophistication and intellectual excitement of Carthage, a university town where pagans and Christians of all kinds mingled, the loss of his father and birth of his son, all before he was twenty, affected Augustine deeply. Intellectually he underwent what has been called a conversion to philosophy, from reading Cicero's *Hortensius* (only partially still extant), and put an abrupt check to the headlong course of his adolescent emotions. The first consequence of this conviction that wisdom was the supreme goal was that Augustine, still a Christian, turned to the Bible to seek it. Disturbed, among other things, by the inconsistency between the two genealogies of Christ set out in the gospels, Augustine soon followed his conversion to philosophy with a conversion to Manichaeism.

This sect, founded a century earlier by Mani (or Manes) in Persia, claimed to be superior to Christianity, many of whose elements it incorporated, and spread widely, even as far as China. The secret and fanatical atmosphere of Manchaean meetings was no doubt an added attraction to the brilliant but immature Augustine, but what struck him most was the Manichaean solution to the problem of evil and human freedom. They taught a fundamental dualism, a God, principle of all goodness, perpetually at war with an equally powerful principle of evil, Light wrestling with Darkness. It is easy to see how eager Augustine would be to attribute the promptings, and not infrequent victory, of sensuality to a baser self, an alien soul, from which his true self, a soul touched with divinity, was absolutely divided. His adolescent sense of guilt was thus neatly explained away. As regards the Bible, too, Manichaean doctrine rejected the vengeful Jehovah as a force quite separate from the true God of mercy. Perhaps the strangest, and certainly the most distinctive, feature of this dualism was that which represented the forces of evil as the active, those of good as the passive elements both in the world and in the individual. As the convert progressed through the ranks of the Manichaean hierarchy of initiation from 'hearer' to 'elect', ever more exacting austerities were demanded of him, so that his good, true, soul might progressively win freedom from the baser self. Augustine was reluctant, probably unable, to take the required step on to election, hence his later recollection of the pathetically reiterated prayer: 'Lord, give me chastity and continence, but not now.'

An immediate consequence of Augustine's conversion to Manichaeism was a bitter quarrel with his mother, who refused for a time to have him under her roof. For a year or so he stayed in Thagaste as a teacher, winning converts to Manichaeism by his zeal, before he returned to Carthage in 376. His twin conversion had made him abandon his parents' earlier plan of a legal career for him in favour of an academic one. In 383, to Monica's great sorrow, Augustine sailed off to Rome in search of wider opportunities.

In Rome he attracted the notice of a powerful patron who, being a pagan, was pleased to be able to nominate the non-Christian Augustine to a chair of Rhetoric in Milan, where the influence of St Ambrose, the Archbishop, had not as yet prevailed. To Milan, therefore, Augustine went in 384, more ambitious than ever, to be joined next year by his mother. Milan, an imperial city then rivalling Rome, offered much scope for advancement, and it was not long before Augustine, now the wrong side of thirty, became betrothed to an heiress as a preliminary to securing some official post which would allow him early and dignified retirement to Africa. The inescapable consequence of this engagement was that he had to dismiss his concubine, who returned to Africa, probably to receive baptism and spend the rest of her life as a religious. Adeodatus remained with his father. While one must be careful to avoid using anachronistic criteria in emotional matters of so remote a period, it is hard to believe that the forcible relegation of a woman with whom he had lived for thirteen years, and her permanent separation from their son, could have been effected without considerable pain, and even guilt on his part. He records his distress at the parting, though apparently in keeping with contemporary usage he never mentions the woman's name, but at this distance in time it is idle to speculate on just what feelings he had about her then or later.

What is certain is that reunited with his devoutly Christian mother, forcibly separated from his mistress, poised on the brink of a successful official career, the emotions of Augustine must have been turbulent and mixed. Through Monica, Augustine was at least in formal contact with Ambrose, involved at the time in a power struggle with Arian heretics enjoying imperial favour, but cannot be said to have come under his influence. Meanwhile his Manichaean convictions were on the wane, and formal but uncommitted acceptance of Catholicism would have been a logical step in his career. One critic writes of him as 'sceptical, disillusioned, but more ambitious than ever'.[1]

Early in 386 Augustine began to read the works of Plotinus and Porphyry, Greek philosophers of the previous century who had rejuvenated the teaching of Plato (hence their name neo-Platonists) in a powerful and original manner. It is now known that Ambrose was also familiar with these works, and sermons of his dating from 386 to 387 clearly show a fusion of Christianity and Platonism which seems to have been much more normal than scholars believed until recently. At all events this reading found Augustine in receptive mood, and is certainly the context, and to some extent the cause, of what happened next.

In August 386 Augustine had begun to have severe attacks of asthma, possibly of psychosomatic origin, which threatened his career as an orator. One day he and a close friend, Alypius, were visited by someone who told them the story of how two unnamed high officials (of whom St Jerome may have been one) had recently been converted while attending the imperial court of Trier. They had come by chance one afternoon upon a small monastery, where they found and read Athanasius' life of the famous hermit, St Antony of Egypt, and were so moved that they instantly decided to follow his example and forsake the world for a monastic life.

As Augustine recounts the episode (in *Confessions* VIII), this example acted at a catalyst. He had been reading St Paul when the visitor arrived, and the story of this sudden conversion at Trier brought home to him his own chronic procrastination when it came to following what he knew to be right. In great anguish of spirit he meditated on the fruits of Continence, whom he personified as addressing him, and bitterly reproached himself for his failure to act. Overcome with tears of contrition he went off alone into the garden to attempt to resolve his problem. Suddenly, he relates, he heard a childish voice from nearby repeating continually the words *'tolle, lege'* (take up, read), and taking this to be some kind of oracle, went back to the place where he had left his friend and the volume of St Paul. Opening the latter he came at once on the words (from Romans 13.13): 'Not in rioting and drunkenness, not in chambering and wantonness, not in strife and envying; but put ye on the Lord Jesus Christ and make not provision for the flesh.' He comments: 'As I came to the end of this sentence, it was as though the light of confidence flooded my heart and all the darkness of doubt was dispelled.'

Modern research has thrown much light on the literary composition of this episode.[2] It is, for instance, very likely that the unknown child's voice alludes to those children of the personified Continence mentioned just before. Again, one MS suggests that the voice may have come not from 'a neighbouring house' (*domo vicina*) as the familiar version has it, but 'from the divine dwelling' (*domo divina*). Fascinating and invaluable as such elucidations are, they do not alter the basic fact that the account in the *Confessions* is the literary expression of an interior event which undoubtedly took place, no doubt at Milan in August 386, but in circumstances we shall never know for certain. All we can do is to look at the subsequent course of Augustine's life and try to assess the nature and cause of the change.

Less than a month after the incident in the garden Augustine withdrew to a place called Cassaciacum (probably near Lake Como) for philosophical retreat, in the company of his mother, his son and a small group of close friends. He resigned his chair of Rhetoric, broke off the intended marriage, and gave himself up to the pursuit of wisdom, this time within a Christian framework. There they all spent the winter, and in March 387 returned to Milan where Augustine, Alypius and Adeodatus, with others, embarked on the lengthy preparations for baptism, living throughout Lent in a kind of secluded novitiate, until 24 April, when they received baptism at the hands of Ambrose. Conversion had been given public and sacramental recognition.

An extant set of dialogues composed at Cassaciacum shows more than anything else intellectual serenity. The incident in the garden had freed Augustine from the bonds of doubt as well as from the tyranny of the senses, and enabled him to recover a sense of purpose. Modern critics stress the fact that Augustine, knowing how such men as St Antony of Egypt turned their backs on culture to seek God in austere solitude, quite deliberately chose the gentler course of combining his newly acquired Christian faith with dedication to a life of philosophical study. Intellectuals throughout the ages have felt the attraction of a fellow intellectual whose conversion in no way dethroned a cultural ideal. At the same time the profoundly intellectual Augustine was no less profoundly emotional; emotional, indeed, about intellectual matters, let alone about passion and human relationships, and it is this dual aspect of his personality that communicates itself with such intensity in so much of his writing.

After his baptism Augustine decided to return home to Africa with his little band. They arrived at the port of Ostia some time in the autumn of 387, but could not sail because of a blockade. While they waited, Monica was taken ill and died after a few days, aged fifty-five. Just before her death she and Augustine shared in a mysterious vision of 'the divine wisdom'. Monica had lived to see her long-cherished conviction that her wayward son would return to the fullness of her faith, and he always felt that she had in some way been instrumental in his conversion.

After burying his mother in Ostia, Augustine returned with the others to wait in Rome until they could at last, in 388, take ship for Africa. They went first to Carthage, and then to Thagaste, where they led a specifically Catholic life of study, combining the Bible and Platonism, in conditions of moderately austere seclusion. Within two years Adeodatus and one of Augustine's inner circle were dead, and he moved on to the final stage of conversion. His contemplative life was becoming lonely, but he was also affected by the religious conflicts of his native province, where Manichaeism was provoking strong Catholic reaction. In 391 he moved to Hippo (later Bône, now Annaba) intending to found a monastery, but before long was compelled by the bishop and his people to accept ordination, a common practice in a church desperately short of worthy volunteers for the priesthood.

The monastery was set up, and produced many African bishops, but Augustine also made a name for himself as a preacher (a function normally reserved in Africa to bishops) and inevitably in 395 was consecrated coadjutor to the Bishop of Hippo, whom he succeeded the following year. Thereafter the story of Augustine's life is that of a tireless writer and preacher, pastor of his flock, defending the Catholic faith against all enemies, Manichaeans, Donatists, Pelagians, and finally succumbing to death in 430 with the Vandals already at the gates.

It is highly significant that the *Confessions* were not begun until 397, when he was already bishop, and that they comprise his spiritual autobiography up to his conversion and the death of Monica, in nine books, followed by four more books of meditation and prayer, reflecting the man he had become in the ten years since his baptism. The complete novelty of the book in its time is masked for us by the many other autobiographical works written since, but in one respect the novelty needs to be underlined. Conversion in the ancient world, down to the time of Augustine, was understood as closing a door on the past, entering upon a new life unmarked by anything that had happened before. Peter Brown, Augustine's outstanding biographer, thus describes the novelty of Augustine's book: 'For Augustine conversion was no longer enough. No such dramatic experience should delude his readers into believing that they could so easily cast off their past identity. The "harbour" of the convert was still troubled by storms.'[3] In other words, the quest for perfection in this life, whether through philosophy, Manichaeism or even Christian neo-Platonism, was as dead as his mother, his son and so many dear friends. Augustine had come to see that evil, within and without, would confront him to the end of his days, but he had more importantly come to acknowledge (*Confessions* X) that in Christ we have a mediator through whom alone we can hope for grace to resist. The 'therapy', as Peter Brown calls it, of the *Confessions* was meant to help him to be a better bishop by learning more about himself and sharing the discovery with others, but also by disclosing and praising God's ways to the man Augustine. The Latin word in fact covers both meanings. No more than the road to Damascus is Augustine's experience normative for all, but for many it became the very type of conversion.

Augustine remained an intellectual to the end of his days, and his writings deal with doctrine in an intellectual way, especially in controversial matters. Moreover his outlook and that of his contemporaries in the later Roman world was totally different from that of St Paul. This no doubt accounts for the abstract, or highly spiritualized, way in which he refers to Christ, more a spiritual concept than a person of flesh and blood, but it does not tell us what his private thoughts and prayers may have been like. The mechanism of grace and redemption is clear enough, as is the reality of sin, but Augustine seems more concerned with divine wisdom and the word than with the cross. We know that the crucifix was unknown in the Africa of his day, and perhaps much that goes with that symbol was equally missing. It is something of a paradox that this most intensely personal of Christian writers should reveal so little of his personal relationship with Christ, but the fact must be recorded.

The third of the great models of conversion comes almost exactly midway between St Augustine and the present day, and represents a peculiarly mediaeval ideal of sanctity. The vast popularity of Francis of Assisi at the present day began rather more than a century ago, and has been accompanied by a no less vast weight of scholarship, not to mention popular literature. It is therefore particularly hard to go back beyond the current picture of the saint, through the earlier picture created and propagated for centuries by his order, to the actual man who lived and died in Assisi nearly eight hundred years ago. Even now there is no general agreement on the detailed chronology of his life, and certainly not on the interpretation of conflicting accounts of his acts and intentions. Yet for millions, rather than thousands, of men and women through the centuries Christianity has had no more authentic exponent since Christ himself than *'il poverello'*, the poor man of Assisi. Much more than Paul, a shadowy figure for all his influence, or the intellectual Augustine, by no means everyone's favourite saint, Francis represents in legend and in fact fundamental truths to which all can respond, with respect if not with allegiance.

His conversion wrought in him a change so total and profound that in the end he literally died of the consequences. That great spiritual historian David Knowles expresses it thus: 'He had begun to know Christ in the reality of living by a supernatural light . . . he saw and followed the life of the gospel, the life of the perfect Christian, in its true simplicity and fullness, not as an ideal, not as a goal, but as the only way of life.'[4] Thus far the story of Francis does not look so very different from that of other true converts, but Knowles goes on to point out the element which proved tragic for Francis and remains an obstacle to any full understanding of him: 'Francis had the mind of Christ, he lived in him, and it was an agony and ultimately an impossibility for him to divide, to adapt and to accommodate for others the unity and fullness of his vision.'

The fullness of that vision did not come to him all at once, nor is it easy to see how much of his later years was implicit in the beginnings, but a spiritual itinerary can be discerned so long as one takes care as far as possible not to read history backwards. It is interesting to see what history made of him after his death, in words and pictures, but it is worth trying to forget history and look at him as a stranger. Almost all the dates that follow are in dispute, sometimes by several years, and even the sequence of some events is obscure, but with those reservations the facts of Francis' life as here described are now generally admitted.

Francis was born in 1181 or 1182 at Assisi in Umbria, one of two sons of Pietro Bernadone, a cloth merchant of substance, and his wife Pica. Pietro's business took him frequently to France, and he was a great admirer of things French, which seems to be the reason for his son's then very unusual name, Francesco, 'the French one'. There is no evidence that Francis ever went to France in his youth, but he learned French songs (probably in the Southern *langue d'oc*) and is often reported talking French for no apparent reason to Italians who did not understand it. A form of Catharism was very much alive at Assisi at the time, and it has been suggested that Pietro may have been sympathetic to that dualist heresy, reminiscent but historically independent of Manichaeism.[5]

Very little is known of Francis' youth. He was educated sufficiently to help his father in the business, but not much more. He was pleasure-loving, sociable and spoilt, typical product of an affluent family dominated by an autocratic father and an indulgent mother. In 1202 he joined his townsmen in a minor war with the neighbouring town of Perugia, was captured in a fierce battle and spent a year in not too rigorous captivity. He was ransomed in 1203 and came home sick in body, possibly with some tubercular infection, and depressed in mind. Probably at about that time he visited Rome, and on an impulse changed clothes with a beggar at St Peter's to see what it felt like to beg alms for a whole day. He is reputed to have been habitually generous to beggars, but this reflects natural kindness and curiosity about a totally alien way of life rather than any considered attitude towards poverty.

In 1205 he decided to join in a campaign going on in the South of Italy under the standard of Walter of Brienne, and set out in search of glory, evidently with his father's approval, since his accoutrements are described as being particularly splendid. The little group from Assisi reached Spoleto for the first night, but next morning Francis was missing. During the night he had heard a voice, as in a dream, telling him to go back home. This was the end of his brief career of chivalry; it cannot have improved his relations with his father, but it was the first sign of a change of heart.

At some unspecified time following the return from Spoleto an incident took place which should probably be regarded as the true beginning of his conversion, because Francis himself refers to it in his Testament of 1226 in an otherwise vague statement about his former worldly life. Francis was always very much a man who lived through his senses, exceptionally alive to the natural world around him, sensitive to all forms of beauty and repelled by ugliness. Lepers, who looked, smelled and sounded extremely unattractive, aroused his special disgust. One day, we read, he was riding along near Assisi when he met a leper by the road; instead of just tossing the man a coin, he dismounted, put the money into the man's hand and kissed it, and then allowed the leper to kiss him in return. Such practical recognition of a fellow human being as a brother in Christ, independent of disease or any other social stigma, would be no light thing for anyone, but for the fastidious Francis it marked a real conquest of self. He followed up this meeting by going several times to the leper hospital just outside the town, giving alms to all the lepers and even tending them. In his own words in the Testament: 'When I was yet in my sins, it seemed to me unbearably bitter to look at lepers. And then the Lord led me into their company and I showed mercy to them. When I went away from them, that which had at first seemed bitter to me was now changed for me into sweetness of soul and body.'[6]

Clearly his abrupt return from Spoleto, however it is to be explained, put an end to one sort of fantasy, that of chivalry and renown, without necessarily putting in its place a sense of reality. The description of the next signpost along Francis' spiritual way makes it clear that the leper incident has a wider context, that stirrings of religious awareness had followed, even perhaps prompted, the Spoleto fiasco. One day Francis was praying before the crucifix (preserved to this day) in the dilapidated church of San Damiano, on the outskirts of Assisi, when the crucified Christ seemed to speak to him: 'Francis, go and repair my church which, as you see, is falling down.'[7] This instruction, which Francis interpreted quite literally, was what he had been waiting for, and determined his way of life for some time to come.

The various biographies of the saint include a number of details of his life at this time which need not be taken at face value, but add up to a picture of indecision, distraction, moodiness, perhaps what modern youth calls an 'identity crisis'. We read of mysterious visits to caves in the neighbourhood in search of some great treasure, inevitably given a spiritual interpretation by the chroniclers, but quite possibly part of Francis' rich fantasy life. One incident occurred when Francis was acting as master of the revels with a band of young merrymakers romping through the town. They suddenly noticed he was no longer with them, and eventually found him standing motionless, as if in a trance. He told them he was overwhelmed by a vision of a bride of surpassing beauty, again inevitably glossed by chroniclers as true religion or poverty, but again perhaps one of his romantic daydreams.

These and similar stories are picturesque illustrations of a state of mind which may well date back to his liberation from Perugia. The aimless pleasure-seeking of his companions satisfied him no more than knightly adventure. He would not even have been tempted to make the gesture to the leper, and then follow it up, unless he had actively begun to heed some inner call. Self-evidently he would not have been praying in San Damiano, or anywhere else, unless he was searching for spiritual guidance and release from uncertainty. Up to then he knew that he was called to some life of quite changed values without knowing specifically what it was, but the leper incident had proved that his will no longer resisted self-denial, and from that moment on he had been ready to obey whatever call might come.

Francis' reaction to the call from the crucified one was typically impulsive and immediate. He went to his father's shop, collected all the bales of cloth he could find, loaded them on a horse and went over to the neighbouring town of Foligno, where he sold the cloth and the horse as well. Returning on foot to San Damiano he offered the money to the embarrassed priest-in-charge, who prudently refused it for fear of what Pietro Bernardone would do. Francis would not take it back, but put it away for safe keeping and asked to be allowed to stay on as a servant of the church, which was accepted.

There is some confusion about what happened next. According to one story Francis hid for a month in a cave, or pit, from his father's wrath, but eventually came out, went home and was there locked up by his father on his obdurate refusal to restore the money. His mother supposedly managed to release him, and he went back to San Damiano. All accounts agree that Pietro, incensed beyond measure by his son's impossible behaviour, summoned Francis before the civil magistrate to face charges of theft and filial disobedience (a statutory offence in Assisi), whereupon Francis successfully pleaded ecclesiastical immunity and was then cited to appear before the bishop.

The scene that ensued, probably in February 1207, was, to say the least, dramatic, and poses some awkward questions. The bishop very properly ordered Francis to return his father's money and find some other way of repairing the church; Francis accepted, and forthwith stripped himself stark naked (the chronicler specifies that he did not even retain his breeches) before the whole assembly. Contemptuously piling the contentious money with all the clothes he owed to paternal expense, Francis publicly repudiated his father, saying that henceforth he would serve only his father in heaven. For decency's sake the bishop covered Francis with his own cloak, and later gave him a servant's discarded clothes. Turning his back on all that had been his life for the past twenty-five years or so, Francis left Assisi in the midwinter snow.

The exhibitionism, the public humiliation of his father, the irresponsibility of the original act, robbing not himself but his father, may have an appeal for those who despise the conventions of a materialistic bourgeoisie, but show a degree of wilfulness and childish petulance, an operatic self-justification at another's expense, that is diametrically opposed to the leper incident. Quite obviously Francis and his father were incompatible, perhaps his father was an evil man; there had to be a break, and it is very likely that the Bernadone household was one in which basic Christian virtues could not be practised. Francis no doubt had to burn his boats, to remove all possibility of reconciliation with his family if he wanted to be free to serve God as he believed he should. None the less, it is hardly the virtue of humility that the naked Francis represents in that spectacular scene.

After drifting not very far north with no very clear idea what to do next, Francis returned some months later to Assisi. This time he set himself the task of repairing San Damiano with his own hands, and with materials begged from anyone willing to help. Apart from one last unedifying clash with his father, who thereafter disappears completely from history, Francis acquired a reputation for harmless, industrious eccentricity, as he begged his food and continued to repair churches. He had ceased to be aimless, had wholly broken with all material values, but was still serving his spiritual apprenticeship. After San Damiano, the abandoned church of San Pietro, after San Pietro that of Santa Maria degli Angeli, better known as the Portiuncula, owned by neighbouring Benedictines, showed the practical results of Francis' conversion. For some two years he was kept physically busy in this way, but if we know nothing of any spiritual insights or development, it must be supposed that he was beginning to wonder whether such a task was all he had been called to.

On St Matthias Day, 24 February, probably 1208, possibly earlier, Francis was hearing mass in the newly restored Portiuncula when the words of the gospel struck him very forcibly: 'As ye go, preach . . . Provide neither gold, nor silver, nor brass for your purses, nor scrip for your journey, neither two coats nor yet staves . . .' (Matthew 10.7–10).[8] After mass he discussed the words and their message with the priest, and suddenly knew that he had found his way: 'This is what I have been wanting; this is what I have been seeking; this is what I long with all my heart to do.' He at once laid aside his shoes, leather girdle and staff, tied a cord round his waist and never again accepted money as alms, refusing even to handle coins. The seed of the original Franciscan rule had been sown.

From being a builder Francis became a preacher of penitence, not at first in anything like sermons, but in simple words and deeds. Within a few weeks he had acquired two or three followers, one a rich man, another a peasant, and it was not long before a dozen of them were living in community in rough huts round the Portiuncula. They would go out in pairs, quite far afield, preaching repentance, doing whatever manual labour was offered, begging their subsistence. None of them was in orders, and they neither claimed nor exercised any authority. Many such groups of lay people, Catholic and heretical, existed at the time, and they were probably conspicuous mainly by the extremity of their poverty and inexperience as preachers.

In 1209 Francis composed a simple rule, now lost, consisting mostly, it seems, of quotations from the Bible such as that which had set him on his path, and intended to be obeyed to the letter. At the suggestion of the Bishop of Assisi the ragged dozen then went to Rome, where after some hesitation due to Francis' unprepossessing appearance and the rigour of the rule, Pope Innocent III approved the rule (which probably already included the name Friars Minor, lesser brothers) and regularized their situation by arranging for them all to be tonsured, and thus brought visibly and officially under clerical jurisdiction. Francis became, and remained, a deacon, but on their return to Assisi a priest, Sylvester, joined them, and they ceased to depend on outsiders for the sacraments. The Franciscan order was born.

Inspiring leader as he was, Francis was no organizer. Thus inevitably the astonishing spread of his order over the next few years imposed great strains on him which eventually, as Knowles says, caused him agony. The spontaneous acceptance of the poorest, humblest place, the simple preaching of the gospel message by men mostly without education, the absolute ban on owning property or buildings, the complete indifference to hardship, above all the uniquely Franciscan spirit of gaiety, the simple joy of the fool (*pazzo*), as Francis called himself, were the main features of the order before it became submerged under the weight of numbers.

The wide geographical dispersion of the Friars Minor reflected Francis' own zeal to preach the gospel far and wide. In 1212 he set off for the Levant, but got no further than Dalmatia. In 1214 he travelled across Spain to Compostella, but was not well enough to continue as intended to Morocco. In 1219 he at last reached Egypt, was present at the capture of Damietta by the Crusaders, and was allowed to cross the lines to interview the Sultan, who received him courteously, listened to him expound Christianity but resisted conversion. From there Francis went on to spend several months in the Holy Land, but was almost certainly unable to visit Jerusalem, then a largely ruined city in enemy hands.

If he had thus satisfied his early desire to be a crusader, Francis returned, probably with some reluctance, in 1220 on receipt of an urgent message to deal with a crisis in the order, which by then numbered perhaps as many as two thousand. A new rule in 1221, another in 1223 (still in force), included concessions forced on Francis partly by dissidents and partly by the inexorable consequences of rapid expansion. He had already appointed a vicar to run the order during his absence in the East, and on his return the controversial Elias, who had come back with him from Acre, became vicar and effective head of the order. Worn out by sickness – he had contracted a severe eye disease, probably trachoma, in the East – weary of argument, all Francis wanted to do was live his life in Christ as he had tried to do ever since his conversion. The order had become a cross for him to bear, and with the recruitment of members from the recently established universities (Paris and Bologna and, from 1224, Oxford) the original prohibition on learning, and on owning, even corporately, books and buildings was bound to lapse. In sorrow he told the Chapter of 1222: 'The Lord told me he wished me to be a new fool in the world, and that he did not want to lead us by any way other than by that wisdom, for by your learning and your wisdom God will confound you.'[9] He was right; within a decade Friars Minor ranked among the leading theologians in Europe, though the resolutely anti-intellectual Francis had done all he could to prevent it.

After the acceptance of the rule in 1223 Francis withdrew from the active government of the order. That year he spent Christmas at Greccio, well south of Assisi, and there constructed a re-enactment of the nativity in a stable with beasts, and an altar at which he served midnight mass as deacon. This is thought to have been the first time the crib was used in Christmas devotions, and shows how deeply absorbed Francis now was in the events of Christ's earthly life. In August 1224 he withdrew with a few friars to still greater solitude at La Verna, or Monte Alverna, a mountain site in Tuscany, well north of Assisi, which he had been given by the local lord some ten years before. There in a rough hut, isolated even from his companions, served once a day by a friar who brought food, Francis spent some weeks in intense prayer and meditation. The subject, and result, of this period of prayer is well known. On 14 September, Holy Cross Day, Francis' prayer, to share Christ's life more fully, was answered: he received the stigmata, marks of the passion, in his hands, feet and side. He seems to be the first person of whom this phenomenon is recorded.

A fortnight later Francis, now very weak, was brought back by stages to Assisi. He insisted on still preaching while he could, but in 1225 an excruciatingly painful operation (the application of a red-hot iron to his temples) failed to save his sight, and he became so ill that he had to spend the winter in Siena, where there were doctors who did their best to ease his pain. Elias somehow brought him back to Assisi in the spring of 1226, and there he wrote his Testament. Finally, on 3 October 1226, lying naked on the ground at the Portiuncula, he died, listening at his own request to a reading of John 13, the account of Christ's reaction to impending death.

The divergencies in the final years, from his departure for the East, between Francis and his order added to his sorrows and may too easily distract attention from his personal development. He had done as he had been bidden at the Portiuncula in 1208, he had gone out to preach repentance in a state of total poverty. Others had soon followed him, so that ten years later he was leading a fully-fledged order with chapters, ministers, provinces and all the other paraphernalia of ecclesiastical organization. Bit by bit, though, the wisdom and learning of his followers prevailed over Francis' holy folly, and the last five years of his life show him leaving the order to run itself while he drew ever closer to Christ in his daily life. It is the reception of the stigmata, not the thousands of friars making up the order, that marks the culminating point of Francis' life, but, of course, the sanctity which found physical expression in the stigmata lived, and lives, on in the order he founded. Even in a man of brilliant intellect like St Bonaventura, Minister General from 1257–74 and often called the second founder of the order, one finds the spirituality of Francis shining out radiantly from several works of great beauty and profundity which contrast strongly with his more technical theological writings.

A characteristic and perhaps unexpected feature of Francis' love for others is to be seen in his many explicit verbal references to maternal care; Francis tells his friars to treat those in their charge with the care of a mother. Compare this with St Benedict, who had given the name 'abbot' (father) to the superior in his rule to symbolize the paternal role. Francis' extraordinary treatment of his own family finds an echo in his frequent and rigid insistence that those willing to leave all and follow him must give their goods to the poor, not to their families, however needy. Conversion seems to have meant for him total severance from all previous attachments, good or bad. Though he continued to live in Assisi, not at all a large town, there is no evidence that he even attended the funeral of his parents. The affective situation in his home quite clearly marked him for life.

For a long time, in varying ways, he saw his call as demanding ceaseless activity in himself, and then in his followers, but it is noteworthy that from the first he made explicit provision for those friars who wished, like him in his later years, to withdraw into some remote place with a few like-minded brethren for a life of prayer and meditation. The constant preaching and travelling were deliberate, but if at the same time Francis had neglected his interior journey, he would never have come to his goal at La Verna. No saint before or since has lived so literally and exclusively the life of Christ, in love and suffering. When death was before him he recognized, and wrote down, that the encounter with the leper twenty years before had been the first step on a road to which he cannot even have suspected the end for years to come.

Legend has richly added to fact, too often obscured it by itself becoming a fact of popular imagination. The beautiful Canticle of the Sun, written soon after the stigmata, bears witness to the love of nature personified in its creatures which lends authority to the stories of his preaching to the birds, taming the wolf and begging Brother Fire to be kind to him as the iron approached his temples. His conversion of St Clare, the rich young girl of Assisi who founded the Second Order (Poor Clares) in 1212, has aroused speculation about their relationship and given rise to romantic legend and sentimental tale. Miracles of healing were freely attributed to him in his lifetime and after his death. The filial devotion of Franciscans (now divided into three main branches) associates their saints and martyrs with their founder. Legend is a way of expressing human reaction to inexplicably great persons and events, and should not be overlooked as one tries to judge Francis' personal impact. In the end, however, one is forced to conclude that all the legend, true or false in origin, is just an attempt to convey to other people, who cannot hope to share the fullness of Francis' vision, how this ragged, physically unimpressive, unlearned deacon from a small Italian town radiated to all he met the inner presence of the Christ with whom he identified even to death.

Paul, Augustine and Francis are so outstanding in every way that inevitably they influenced countless other converts, sometimes by providing literary models for recitals of later conversions. They by no means exhaust the categories of conversion, but they are so different one from another, so memorable and so famous, that it is useful to remember the experiences they had and related when one looks at more recent converts. These three, together with innumerable others, helped to build up in the first fifteen hundred years of Christianity certain norms, even expectations, which provide the context for the more faithfully recorded stories of the past four or five hundred years. Parallels and analogies will inevitably suggest themselves in the chapters that follow, but these will only be examined in detail when all the evidence has been presented. Meanwhile these three great models serve to remind us of the variety and coherence of Christian experience through the ages.

2

MARTIN LUTHER

It may seem to be begging the question to call Luther a convert at all, let alone a convert from error to truth, but his experience is so integral a part of the Protestant tradition and has since been paralleled so often, that there is at the very least a *prima facie* case for investigating the proposition that he underwent one (or perhaps more) of those experiences generally called conversion. The historical consequences of Luther's spiritual development must be rigorously set aside in trying to assess what actually happened to Luther himself: even with hindsight it cannot be maintained that in human terms the effects of his actions must inevitably have been what they were, and no one questions Luther's own assertion that he neither intended nor foresaw them. This is not to deny that certain attitudes to providence, or to historical determinism, may radically condition one's judgment of men and events, and that in dealing with religion it may even be unrealistic to ignore such attitudes, but the examination of the case is a legitimate enterprise in its own right, regardless of the lessons to be drawn from or applied to it.

Martin Luther was born in 1483 into a family of what he describes as peasants; his father later became a miner, and then an official of some substance in Mansfeld, Thuringia. Lucas Cranach's portrait confirms the general impression that Luther's father was an authoritarian, even hard, man, and Martin was brought up in no doubt as to where his duty lay. Fear of parental disapproval, reinforced by corporal punishment, formed part of the boy's early experience, but while this is consistent with his later attitude to God and authority in general, there is no need to see the connection as being necessary or definitive.

After attending various schools, Luther began his studies at Erfurt University in 1501, intending to take up a career in the law. He records of this period that he was already subject to fits of depression, accompanied by feelings of sin and guilt, but all the evidence suggests that he led a blameless life by any standards. His father's demands, personal religious scruples, and physiological factors, no doubt all contributed to his character in varying degrees, but it is certain that tensions existed in him from an early age which were not resolved in the normal course of adolescence. His studies progressed satisfactorily, and his father no doubt confidently expected that a lucrative future awaited him, when quite suddenly, in July 1505, Martin joined the Augustinian Hermits (despite the name, one of the orders of mendicant friars) at Erfurt. The documentary facts are not in dispute, nor is his father's furious reaction to what was obviously a sudden decision, but, of course, the real motives and events behind the decision are only known to us by Luther's own account, written some fifteen years later, when he already regretted what he had done. To that extent the inevitably edited recollections of the past cannot be wholly above suspicion, but there is no intrinsic reason for dismissing them.

In 1521 he dedicated to his father a book on monastic vows, and there states: 'I had been called by terrors from heaven and became a monk against my own will and desire . . . I had been beleaguered by the terror and agony of sudden death, and I made my vows perforce and of necessity.'[1] This much is reasonably certain; had it been otherwise his father would not have failed to make it known. Behind the cryptic words lies a circumstantial story, or two, to be more precise, which may not be the whole or literal truth but, having the force of legend, at least shows what Luther wanted others to believe, what he had probably come to believe himself, and what in the last analysis may not have been too far from the truth. He recalls how he was caught in a violent thunderstorm on a road some way from Erfurt and 'had been so shaken by a flash of lightning that he had cried out in terror, "Help me, St Anne, and I will become a monk." '[2] Two weeks later, to the anger of his father and dismay of his friends, he fulfilled the vow. 'I never dreamed of leaving the monastery. I had quite died to the world.' The second story involves an accident, again on a country road far from assistance, when he wounded himself with his own sword seriously enough to fear that he might bleed to death. Legend or not, encounters with the fact of death in a violent and plague-ridden age were frequent and inescapable.

In some sense the commitment to monastic life must be called a conversion. Whatever he later came to believe about vows in general and his own in particular, he did leave the world, with the prospect, he tells us, 'of an honourable and wealthy marriage' arranged by his father and a career to match. He was by universal consent a good monk, active and conscientious, and from his entry into the monastery until his death his life was explicitly devoted to the service of God. However the occasion of the vows may be interpreted, his change of life, in that sense 'conversion', was due to fear, to feelings of sin and guilt rendered intolerable by the threat of sudden death, followed by judgment, and this spiritual disposition did not change. None the less, as a sudden decision, breaking with an existing and expected pattern, maintained over fifteen years or so, Luther's entry into religion may properly be accounted an initial conversion.

The life on which he now embarked was as well equipped as any to allay his fears. A supportive community, a full timetable, serious study and teaching, wise and compassionate superiors and advisers, limitless opportunity for confession and spiritual counsel, all this brought him no nearer to real peace of mind and seems even to have sharpened his apprehension of hell. A striking example of his state of mind is his account of his first mass after ordination to the priesthood in 1507. As he reached the central and most solemn prayers of the Canon he was seized with such dread that he found it hard to continue. At the festive meal that followed, his father in a sudden burst of anger queried the validity of a vocation undertaken in defiance of the commandment to honour one's parents. Although the description of the incident was not recorded until much later, by which time it had taken on a different significance, there is no reason to doubt its essential accuracy.

The next milestone in his career, which may be said to mark his definitive conversion, cannot be dated with any certainty, and as more evidence comes to light, so scholars produce new and conflicting arguments in favour of this or that moment. Luther himself is quite specific as to what set him on his new and decisive course, and in conversations dating from 1532, 1538, 1542, and finally in a strange autobiographical fragment, written shortly before his death, in 1545, disclosed the insight that changed his life. Only in the last account does he assign it to the year 1519.[3] Because the moment of truth apparently occurred when he was in a tower, forming part of the monastery at Wittenberg (and according to one not quite impossible version in a room there

36 Conversion

used as a privy), the experience and the theology it generated
have come to be known as the *Turmerlebnis* (tower experience).
Apart from the obvious polemical potential of the location (and
presumed occupation) of Luther at this memorable moment, it is
of no importance where he had it, though it is of considerable
importance for proper exegesis of his earlier work to know when
(and, conversely, such exegesis is the main basis for any dating).
The most recent work on this problem suggests that a major
spiritual experience, possibly dramatized by Luther in later
recollections, was the starting point for a quite lengthy process of
intellectual insight, culminating in 1519.[4] At all events, the con-
sistency of all Luther's accounts shows conclusively what happened, if not just how, and over what period of time.

The key to Luther's spirituality, and probably to what should
be seen as the authentically Protestant outlook ever since, is the
notion of justification. While it is easy enough to give an intellectual account of what this means, the emotional and spiritual
implications for Luther and his contemporaries were so radically
different from what later became the case, that it is essential to
set and judge his doctrine in its historical context. In technical
terms the predominant doctrine in the late Middle Ages was a
works-theology, by which salvation depended upon the merits of
the sinner, constituted by accomplishing works of piety and suitable sacramental discipline. Intercessory prayer was a major task
of monks (in theory, at any rate), and innumerable foundations,
from modest chantry chapels to such places as All Souls' College
at Oxford, testify to the universal respect in which after-life insur-
ance was held. The almost frenetic multiplication of devotional
exercises invited a mechanical, quantitative approach to piety: the
rosary devotion, pilgrimages, relics, indulgences, wearing of habits
or scapulars by laymen are all different ways in which the late
mediaeval church encouraged people to earn, and even purchase,
salvation. There can never be rest for the unquiet conscience
while the possibility of earning still further merit remains obsti-
nately present, and one can see how destructive must have been
the combination of a sense of guilt with outwardly blameless
monastic life. Luther wanted nothing less than assurance, and no
humanly devised methods brought him within reach of it. The
stumbling-block was the idea of the righteousness, *justitia*, of God,
and especially the formulation in Romans 1.17: 'For therein [the
gospel] the righteousness of God is revealed from faith to faith.'
Luther's own words are clear and compelling: 'However irre-
proachable my life as a monk, I felt myself in the presence of God

to be a sinner with a most unquiet conscience, nor could I believe him to be appeased by the satisfaction I could offer. I did not love – nay, I hated this just God who punishes sinners. . . '[5]

Psychologists, amateur and professional, have made much of the emphasis on placating, on punishment, on the stern father-figure of a God whose standards are never to be met, and it would be as wrong to dismiss their comments as it would be to accept them as a sufficient explanation of Luther's doctrines. He was in a spiritual impasse, and so long as he saw salvation in terms of human merit he was condemned to endless torment, here and hereafter. The break came, he tells us, when he was pondering (in the tower) the next words of Romans, 'the just shall live by faith', and it occurred to him in a flash of light that the *justitia* was given by God to *justify* and not exercised to *judge*. The sinner will always be a sinner, but he is at last released from the hopeless quest for merit through works. 'In thy sight shall no man living be justified', but by God's saving grace through faith all may hope for salvation.

It is very hard today to appreciate the crippling burden of fear and guilt of which Luther thus divested himself. The injunction to believe, to put all one's trust in God and none in oneself, to rest secure in the sacrifice of the cross made once and for all, did not absolve the sinner from effort, far from it, nor, as opponents claimed, was it in any way antinomian, but it removed at a stroke the bondage of the Law (performance of works) and the illusion that human effort, if only heroic enough, must prevail against sin. One of Luther's favourite illustrations of the doctrine as he now saw it was the parable of the good Samaritan, where Christ, the Samaritan, *justified* the sinner, the victim, at the inn, in other words used his merit as guarantee for the payment of which the beneficiary, disabled by sin, was incapable.

Put in such terms Luther's discovery does not sound very revolutionary, and he soon afterwards found that St Augustine had similarly interpreted the doctrine of justification, thus providing a powerful defence, especially in his own order, against any charges of innovation. He knew, however, that if justification by faith were adopted in preference to the existing works-theology, not only practices and institutions but persons and attitudes would have to be radically changed. Perhaps the most important fact about his discovery was the context in which he made it. In his own psychological and spiritual terms it provided him with a desperately needed release from a mental block, and thus supplied the emotional impetus for further progress. In terms of communicating to others this essentially private experience, however, the intellectual basis of the discovery, and its social application, were far more powerful.

On the European scene, Erfurt and Wittenberg were not specially influential towns or universities, nor did the Saxon province of the Augustinian Hermits enjoy particular prestige, but the familiar picture of Luther, the obscure friar from a relatively uncultured region, has two sides to it. What he was, and what he did, makes sense only in the light of what was successively possible, desirable and necessary.

First his monastic career: under the wise and humane guidance of Johann Staupitz, then Provincial of the order, young Brother Martin was gently steered away from his disaster-course to a more hopeful view of Christianity. As one critic puts it, Staupitz saved him from a nervous breakdown and 'enabled Luther to relax to look at Christ on the cross, not on the judgment seat'.[6] This view, relating to the early years in the monastery, is clearly correct, but the later breakthrough would not have been necessary if Staupitz had been wholly successful. As it was, Staupitz was also responsible for setting Luther, against his inclinations, to take the doctorate in theology, and embark on a teaching career at Wittenberg, the university newly established by the Elector Frederick the Wise, and briefly at Erfurt. There can be no doubt whatever that the exacting preparation of lecture courses before very live audiences on specific books of scripture gave Luther the opportunity to work things out for himself intellectually and the technique for communicating his findings to others. He early became a major figure in Wittenberg; through Spalatin, the Elector's chaplain, he won his ruler's respect and confidence, and within his own order his reputation for learning and reliability extended over most of Germany. From the somewhat supercilious viewpoint of Paris, let alone Rome, these were modest enough qualifications, but for Luther himself, child of the soil that he was, his power-base was solid, secure and eminently worthy. Germans had recently begun to take themselves seriously in matters of culture, and their always sturdy nationalism had little use for the reputedly degenerate Italians or frivolous French. From the first Luther was a prophet honoured in his own land.

In that connection, the excessive emotionalism with which he has so often been taxed, not without cause, must be balanced by his highly respectable intellectual gifts. Ever since Erasmus in the first decade of the century had begun to win a European reputation, humanists north of the Alps had been as active and effective as those in Italy. Reuchlin, the Hebraist (and great-uncle of Philip Melanchthon, Luther's gifted lieutenant); Erasmus himself, whose Greek New Testament (1515) changed the exegetical map; Ulrich von Hutten, satirist, scholar and associate of the knightly brigands of Franconia and the Rhine; the Dominican Eck, later to be Luther's main opponent; and countless others had helped Germans acquire newly purified Latin, and above all Greek and Hebrew for serious biblical study. Luther taught himself Greek and some Hebrew, but more importantly could draw on the latest sound humanist scholarship for his scriptural interpretation. It was as a professional theologian and biblical scholar, not just as a man spiritually tormented, that he approached the problems of faith.

He relates his excitement at the discovery that the familiar Latin word of the Vulgate, *poenitentia*, with its inseparable penal connotations, is rendered in the original Greek *metanoia*: 'change of heart'. The confidence of these sixteenth-century exegetes may today seem excessive, and in the light of subsequent work certainly premature, but there is no gainsaying the shock, and relief, provoked by their removal of centuries-old misunderstandings based on mistranslation. A. G. Dickens goes so far as to say: 'Luther's interpretation of Christianity depended on how one translated certain Greek words',[7] and Luther himself, referring to his commentary on Psalms (1519), wrote: 'Our first concern will be for the grammatical meaning, for this is the truly theological meaning.'

It seems to follow, therefore, that whatever the source of his tower experience, it was tested and then buttressed by competent, close study of scripture according to the methods and principles newly made available by humanists. It is an open question whether fresh linguistic or literary evidence would have made him change his mind, because such evidence, even if available, could hardly have been conclusive on the basic issue of justification. It is beyond doubt that Luther meant what he said when in his successive confrontations with authority he declared himself ready to recant when, but only when, he was proved wrong by scripture. His certainty came from an alliance of heart and mind, from a conscience at last pacified and articulated by intellectually rigorous arguments suitable for transmission to others less learned, and probably less distressed. He was not so much converted to as by the doctrine of *Scriptura sola* (scripture alone), for this gave him the objective criterion so necessary for countering the excesses of sectaries given to anarchical enthusiasm.

After a journey to Rome on business connected with his order

(1510 or 1511), Luther began the series of lectures at Wittenberg the surviving manuscript notes of which are the principal sources for charting his spiritual development. The first course (1513–14) was on Psalms, and one modern scholar claims to have identified the precise place and moment of Luther's insight into justification as early as this. Next he went on to Romans (1515–16), where his thought, now nourished by Augustine, directly confronted the doctrine of justification. The majority of scholars place the crucial breakthrough before, rather than after, this second lecture course, but recognize that the definitive lineaments of Protestantism are still far from drawn. For the latter part of it he read Erasmus' Greek New Testament, and throughout, and thenceforth, constantly referred to St Augustine's teaching on sin. After Romans he went on to Galatians (1516–17, revised in 1519 and again in 1531), describing it as his favourite work. This epistle, with its emphasis on the dangers of the Law, afforded Luther ample opportunity for denouncing the theology of works.

The chronology and significance of the next event, the posting of 95 theses on the door of the Castle church at Wittenberg, on 31 October 1517, are not in dispute. A clash was bound to come sooner or later between Luther and the representatives of official works theology, but it was fortuitous, and fortunate for Luther, that the occasion should be a particularly blatant abuse of the already dubious practice of hawking indulgences for sale. Retracing the chain of causality back from the definitive schism, it is undeniably true that the 95 theses and the ensuing controversy mark the beginning of a continuous line of protest culminating in what is now called Protestantism, but many similar protests over the centuries had resulted variously in recantation, suppression or even reform, and it is absurd to suppose that in 1517 Luther even entertained the idea of a breakaway church, still less one led by him. He was making a protest in due form, he was offering to defend against all comers 95 theses, mostly concerned, directly or indirectly, with indulgences, and also questioning papal authority in this domain, but for debate, not as dogma, and he was observing protocol by sending copies to his diocesan bishop and to the Archbishop of Mainz, Albrecht of Brandenburg, who, we now know, had been promised the major share of the proceeds of selling indulgences to pay off his debts. As theses for debate they were a non-event; no one took up the challenge, but very soon German, as well as Latin, copies were circulating widely and provoking vigorous reaction from both friend and foe.

Whether or not any act of piety, or cash contribution, can

secure remission of punishment for souls in purgatory (that is, indulgence), no one will ever know for certain in this life, but whether or not the cause of piety was advanced by the flamboyant commercialism and extravagant claims of the Dominican Tetzel, commissioned to preach indulgences in Saxony, is hardly controversial. The Pope needed money to build St Peter's, the Archbishop of Mainz needed money to pay off his bankers, and if they could colour their profits with a tincture of devotion, so much the better. Luther might equally well have chosen the sale of relics, or exploitation of pilgrims (Wittenberg had a spectacular collection of relics, attracting considerable tourist revenue), or simony, or what you will, but in the event he chose indulgences as the target for his attack.

Apart from the crude financial interests vested in the practice, the authority of the Pope to promulgate doctrines with no apparent scriptural warrant, and no respectable oral tradition, was now publicly at stake. The issue of indulgences was theologically negotiable, the challenge to authority was not. It is at this point that the depth and solidity of Luther's convictions become clear, and decisive. As Luther's cause was taken up by a wide variety of people mainly united in their resentment at Roman abuses – humanists, German nationalists, genuine reformers – the authorities were obliged to take strong action. First, in October 1518, Luther was summoned to appear at Augsburg before Cardinal Cajetan (the Dominican, Thomas de Vio), an outstanding exponent of Thomist theology and an austere enemy of abuses. The issues at this meeting were principally those of indulgences and the necessity of faith in the recipient for making sacraments efficacious. The meetings ended angrily, Luther feeling that he had been patronized, Cajetan that he had been insulted. Perhaps for the first time Luther, and others, began to realize just what was at stake, and the eventual support of the Elector Frederick probably tipped the scales at this stage. Without political support Luther could hardly have continued his defiance without being arrested and probably executed.

Next year, in July 1519, there was at last a full-scale public debate, at Leipzig, between the robust Eck, another Dominican, and Luther, theoretically assisting his senior Wittenberg colleague Carlstadt. The issue of indulgences and purgatory naturally came up, but it had already become secondary to that of authority. By now Luther's attitude was hardening; he not only challenged papal supremacy, alleging it to be the invention of Sylvester (died 335), but even claimed that the Council of Constance (1415) had erred in condemning at least some of the propositions of John Huss, the Bohemian reformer burned at the stake as a result. This was unquestionably heresy, and equally distasteful to papalists and conciliarists (the significant number of Catholics who put the authority of a properly convened general council above that of the Pope), but on the single point of authority, not on Catholic doctrine as such. J. M. Todd maintains that as late as spring 1519 Luther did not think of schism, 'he is still sure that his own theology and the criticisms he has made remain essentially within the bounds of Catholic Christian tradition',[8] and he is almost certainly right. If such was Luther's view, it could not survive the inexorable workings of the machine now set in motion against him by the Pope himself.

Leo X had had enough, and on 15 June 1520 published the Bull *Exsurge Domine*, condemning a list of forty articles allegedly held by Luther against orthodox teaching. Luther's answer was in the form of three pamphlets rejecting all compromise, and going much further than before. In his address 'To the Christian Nobility of the German Nation', he contemptuously denies the Pope any authority, preaching the priesthood of all believers. In the 'Babylonish Captivity of the Church' he reduces the number of sacraments from seven to three: baptism, penance and eucharist (defined in a very different way from the Catholic doctrine of transubstantiation). In 'Concerning Christian Liberty' he states categorically, 'One thing and one alone is necessary for life, justification and Christian liberty; and that is the most holy word of God, the gospel of Christ', and 'this is that Christian liberty, our faith, the effect of which is, not that we should be careless or lead a bad life, but that no one should need the law or works for justification and salvation.'[9] Protest had recognizably become Protestantism.

The last act was the most solemn, and by now a foregone conclusion. Before the Emperor Charles V and the Imperial Diet at Worms, on 18 April 1521, Luther refused to recant, and ended his speech with the words: 'Unless I am convicted by the testimony of scripture or plain reason . . . I am bound by the scriptures I have quoted, and my conscience is captive to the word of God. I neither can nor will revoke anything, for it is neither safe nor honest to act against one's conscience.'[10] The legendary 'Here I stand, I can do no other' is a later emendation, but serves its lapidary purpose in history.

At Augsburg, at Leipzig and finally at Worms, Luther had been in real physical danger, and only accepted the respective meetings when a safe-conduct had been provided. The grim example of Huss, burned despite such a safe-conduct, left Luther in no doubt as to the risks he ran. It is in these encounters, especially the last, that the nature and effects of his conversion from the old scholastic system to what was now becoming a new system of his own show forth most clearly. On the way to Worms he received a hero's welcome at Erfurt, and referred to it as his Palm Sunday. R. H. Fife writes: 'Quite naively in his own mind he parallels his Worms adventure to Christ's entry into Jerusalem, and his trial and crucifixion. Now in deadly seriousness he wonders whether his pompous entry into the university city [Erfurt] was a temptation of the devil or a sign that his own death was approaching.'[11] At Worms he was literally one man against imperial and Roman authority. Failure or recantation would have been irrevocable, but no one could, or did, foresee the consequences of steadfastly maintaining his stand on scripture and conscience. That word of God which had freed him, however many years before, from the terrors of the Law also held him, as he said, captive now. The destruction of his body was as nothing to the spiritual destruction which recantation would have entailed. Inevitably his physical survival was taken by him and his followers as a sign of divine approval, and as further proof that the Pope and all his works were indeed Antichrist. It is, of course, true that his martyrdom would have been consistent with the same thesis.

The formal breach with Rome was sealed with the Bull *Decet Romanum*, of January 1521, apparently not received at Worms until the end of April. By this Bull Luther, his followers, and anyone giving them aid or comfort was excommunicated. Schism was official. There remained some important steps before anything resembling a Lutheran church came into being.

On the way back from Worms Luther was abducted (by prior arrangement with the Elector) and kept for his own safety for eight months at the Wartburg, a castle in Thuringia. Frederick was thus enabled to keep his word to Luther without openly defying the ban which made him an outlaw. During this time of enforced inactivity Luther was beset by doubts – *Anfechtungen*, as he called them, attacks of temptation – as to the rightness of his conduct, but the period of consolidation was spiritually beneficial. It also enabled him to write a lot, and above all to put the Bible into German. In a real sense the word of God known to Lutherans ever since has been Luther's word, probably the greatest single influence on the German language of all time.

Meanwhile, disquieting news reached him from Wittenberg,

where Carlstadt's enthusiasm was rapidly leading to radicalism and anarchy. Against the Elector's wishes Luther returned in 1522, abandoning the secular disguise he had worn at the Wartburg, and, dressed once more in his Augustinian habit, took over the cause of reformation at Wittenberg, preaching a series of sermons which restored order. Strangely, he continued to wear his habit until 1524, and only took the irrevocable step of marriage, to Catharina von Bora, a former Cistercian nun, in 1525, seemingly because she was finding it hard to make a suitable match and he felt some responsibility for nuns who returned penniless to the world as a result of his teaching. She, and five of their children, survived him, and he died in 1546 secure in the love of his family.

The course of the twenty-five years from Worms to his death showed many, even gross, errors of judgment, and ceaseless activity in writing, preaching, teaching the word of God. The complex political situation in the German lands made Luther an arbiter rather than an authority in secular matters, and even more so in religious ones. His savage condemnation of the Peasants' Revolt, and of the sectaries, shows him ruthlessly sitting on the lid of the Pandora's box he had unwittingly opened. His bitter disagreement over the theology of the eucharist, first with Zwingli, then with Calvin, shows him as unbending in his dogmatism as the Scholastics with whom he had parted company. His violence, obscenity and obsessive contempt for enemies, Roman or anti-Roman, is unattractive and uncompromising. Though marriage and the final abandonment of all monastic constraints made him more human in his enjoyment of normal carnal pleasures, perhaps drinking to excess in good company, he did not become more relaxed in controversy. He had not faced death, incurred excommunication and outlawry, only to admit later that he might have been wrong.

In the last analysis, the Reformation as it came about is a vast inverted pyramid of which the apex and foundation is Luther's conscience, Luther's faith and Luther's translation of the word of God; he was sure, he could do no other, and people looked up to him to give them assurance. There is no doubt that some reformation was bound to happen, but we can only be concerned with that which actually did happen. It cannot be stressed too much that every single person who followed Luther in his own day could only do so by breaking visibly with a church established for centuries, by rejecting vows and sacraments, an international institution and supernatural promises. J. M. Todd, himself a convert to Catholicism, writes: 'Luther never became anything like an "enthusiast" . . . He did not believe in a private revelation to himself, or in the arrival of some special dispensation over and above what is to be expected at all times throughout the life of the church.'[12] Gordon Rupp, a Protestant, adds another dimension: 'He lived on the edge of time, and believed that the Papacy was just another human institution swollen in arrogance and power, and now toppling to its doom, the engine of Antichrist. This was worse than a crime; it was a mistake.'[13] Many, including Catholics, would now add that the Roman church, by seeing Luther as just one more of an endless line of heresiarchs, committed a blunder no less grave.

The necessity to escape from an intolerable spiritual predicament brought Luther the revelation of justification by faith; the application of that doctrine led him to condemn the abuse of indulgences and the system of authority which sanctioned them; the failure of his opponents to refute his case from scripture left him no choice but to maintain and elaborate it; and, finally, when the church as then constituted cast him out, he could only conclude that it was no longer the church of Christ. His call was to believe in the word and follow it, if need be to death, and the political and historical context thrust on him a leadership he had never sought or even imagined. Not even the prospect of a united reformed church, doctrinally and politically aligned against Rome, could make him concede anything to other Protestant leaders. Certainty was for him indivisible; all that others had to do was to submit – not to him personally, but to the word of God of which his conscience remained captive to the end.

3

IGNATIUS LOYOLA

The name of St Ignatius Loyola is so inseparably associated with that of the Society of Jesus which he founded that it is extraordinarily hard to see the man except through the distorting prism of his spiritual sons and their history. Jesuits remain among the most characteristic products of the Counter-Reformation; their intellectual standards and their involvement in ecclesiastical politics make them probably the single most influential body within the Catholic church; and if, in a very real way, they continue to derive inspiration from their founder, they stand individually and collectively in marked contrast to the man Ignatius. It is not just a question of institutionalizing, and so changing, an individual insight, as perhaps his followers did in the case of Francis of Assisi, but rather of setting a final crystallization of vision, as embodied in the Society's Constitutions, against the long and almost incoherent process leading up to it. In a word, the raw material of Ignatius' life bears, at first sight, little or no resemblance to the finished product represented by his order. The clue, indeed the only explanation, lies in his conversion experience and its chain of consequences.

Like so many of his contemporaries, Ignatius was very vague about the year of his birth but, despite persisting uncertainty, scholars favour 1491. He was born Inigo, and only took the Latinate form Ignatius (in fact of quite different origin) much later, but to avoid confusion he will be here referred to throughout by the more familiar Ignatius. His birthplace was the castle of Loyola, in the Basque province of Guipuzcoa, where his family held noble rank. His native tongue was Basque, a fact which some Spanish scholars have claimed to be responsible for his rather clumsy

Spanish style. About eight or nine children had already been born to his parents, and his mother died very soon after giving birth to Ignatius. In 1507, when the boy was about sixteen, his father, Beltran, died, but for a variety of reasons Ignatius had not stayed in the family home, receiving part of his education in Castile, where, of course, he had to speak Spanish, so that he must have been fairly independent of paternal influence even before losing his father. In 1520 Juan Velasquez, his Castilian host, fell into royal disfavour and the young Ignatius took service with the Duke of Nájera. He was not primarily a soldier, though he inevitably took part in some real fighting, and it would be more realistic to see him as a courtier able to perform the military duties expected of any able-bodied young noble of the day.

Evidence concerning this early period consists largely of much later recollections, and cannot be assessed with complete accuracy, but there is no reason to doubt that a good-looking, personable young aristocrat, recently orphaned, would have acquired worldly habits at an impressionable age, that this would have involved more or less serious adventures with women, and that he would scarcely have bothered to recall his addiction to such romances as that of Amadis of Gaul unless it had been genuine. As is so often the case, the available evidence suggests frivolity rather than wickedness, lack of serious purpose rather than blind selfishness.

In May 1521, when he must have been about thirty, Ignatius found himself on campaign in Navarre, territory currently in dispute between Spain and the dispossessed King of Navarre, backed by the French. Besieged in the fortress of Pamplona in an engagement so insignificant that it almost escaped the notice of historians, Ignatius inspired his comrades to hold out against all hope, until he was suddenly wounded so severely in the legs by a stray cannonball that the fortress surrendered.

He immediately underwent clumsy and ineffectual surgery, was transported to Loyola in extreme pain and suffered two more operations, and was unusually fortunate in such circumstances to keep his leg, with only a limp to betray the months of excruciating pain and immobility. It was the latter, much more than the former, to which he owed the first stages of his conversion. Like many another bedridden patient he preferred entertainment to edification, but for some reason the library (if one can call it that) at Loyola held none of his favourite romances in stock, so he had to make do with what there was. For the nine or so months of convalescence he had no other books to read than the *Life of*

Christ by the fourteenth-century Carthusian, Ludolph of Saxony, and a Spanish version of the *Golden Legend*, the immensely popular compilation of saints' lives by the thirteenth-century Jacob of Voragine.

According to his own later account, he was specially impressed by St Francis of Assisi, less expectedly by the Egyptian hermit Onuphrius, and he began to want to go to Jerusalem. What he called a vision of Mary and the child Jesus filled him with such loathing for his past life, and especially for his 'carnal indulgence', that he seemed thenceforth to be delivered from 'all the sinful imagery formerly in his mind'. He is probably referring to romantic daydreams of beautiful women inspired by *Amadis* (and no doubt by actual women, too), because there are such allusions among the memories of his worldly life. In this frame of mind he made enquiries about two of the strictest orders in Spain, the Cistercians and Carthusians, and for a time thought of joining the latter on his eventual return from Jerusalem. It is hard to say just how he saw his future at this stage, but his vision was certainly an idealistic, even romantic, one, and he may well have seen himself as a kind of knight errant in the spiritual army of Christ, without really translating such a view into any practical terms.

By the end of February 1522 his leg and general health were sufficiently restored for him to leave his brother's hospitality at Loyola, though as yet no one else knew what he had in mind. He made his way right across Spain to the Catalan abbey of Montserrat. There he gave away his mule and his good clothes, exchanging with those of a beggar, made a lengthy general confession, and kept a vigil all night for the Feast of the Annunciation. As a further symbol of his new life he hung up the sword and dagger of his former chivalrous calling as *ex votos*. Like so many converts, he knew now that he had irrevocably abandoned his old life, its privileges as much as its sins, but he had little if any idea of what to do next.

In the event, after the first mass of the day (25 March), he made his way to the not very important town of Manresa, also in Catalonia, where he began to lead a life of prayer and extreme physical austerity. At first he lived in a hospice, later in quarters attached to the Dominican house, practising strict abstinence from food and drink, and on one occasion going for a whole week without taking anything at all. At Montserrat for the first time he had confided his spiritual problems to a confessor (a French Benedictine with a reputation for sanctity) and during his ten months or so at Manresa continued to do so, going to confession and communion regularly every week. At Montserrat he had been recommended the spiritual exercises of a recent abbot, Cisneros, and at Manresa he encountered the *Imitation of Christ*, the most widely read devotional book of all time, both expressions of the rather simple piety of the *devotio moderna* movement, which had originated in the Netherlands in the late fourteenth century.

It is universally agreed that the foundations of Ignatius' spirituality were laid at Manresa, and that the main lines of all he subsequently wrote can be traced back to the experience of these months of trial. It is very much less clear exactly what that experience was, not least because Ignatius' own later account is so elusive.[1] Some of the points he makes are straight-forward enough. He began to be tormented by scruples about sins he might have omitted to confess, but was eventually convinced by his obviously sensible confessor that he must put the past right out of his mind. His dangerous excesses of fasting were likewise brought under control, thanks again to his confessor. He tells us that after about four months at Manresa he passed through an acute depressive crisis, with suicidal temptations, and that some kind of alternating manic-depressive phase followed. From the beginning of his stay at Manresa, when he deliberately neglected his physical appearance, cutting neither hair nor nails (he was normally most fastidious), he began to have strange visions ('the form of a serpent with many things that shone like eyes') which brought him consolation.

Read in cold blood, these and similar details are not reassuring. Such unaccustomed fasting and lack of sleep, such intense devotional concentration by one previously unversed in the spiritual life, might well be expected to produce depressive crises and hallucinations, but much of the reader's unease undoubtedly comes from the inadequacy of the narrative. Replaced in the context of Ignatius' whole spiritual development these phenomena can be seen as crude symptoms of a bitter struggle for a new spiritual identity, freed from all the selfishness and vanity of the previous thirty years. He says himself that in these bewildering experiences he came to recognize the 'diversity of spirits' and thus practise that discernment which became a corner-stone of Ignatian spirituality.

Whatever one may think of the serpentine vision, there are others of much greater importance and much clearer meaning, which have nothing in common with visual hallucination. In his chapter on Manresa he lists five points to illustrate how God was patiently instructing him like a teacher with a backward boy. He briefly describes in turn how he 'saw' the inner truth of the Trinity, of creation, of Christ's real presence in the eucharist and of Christ's humanity (twenty or forty times).

The fifth and last of these points is the decisive one. By the banks of the river Cardoner he sat down one day to meditate. 'When he was seated the eyes of his understanding began to be opened; though he did not see any vision, he understood and knew many things, both spiritual things and matters of faith and of learning, and this was with so great an enlightenment that everything seemed new to him. Though there were many, he cannot set forth the details that he understood then, except that he experienced a great clarity in his understanding.' He goes on to say that the total of things he knew and the assistance God gave him over the next thirty years added together 'would not amount to as much as he had received at that one time'.

Such formal testimony leaves no room for doubt as to the effect of the experience, but unfortunately leaves a great deal of room for speculation as to its content. Though he had other visions throughout his life, and other moments of crisis and uncertainty, the period of Manresa and the Cardoner revelation in particular represented a process which resulted in conversion to a specific way of life and a validation of that way when he later attracted others to follow him. It is thus partly in the subsequent course of his life and partly in the written works, especially the *Autobiography* and *Exercises*, of later years that both the content and effect of Manresa can best be seen.

It must be remembered that Ignatius set out from Loyola with one clear goal: Jerusalem. But this geographical destination was also a spiritual one and could be reached only by way of Montserrat and Manresa. However overwhelming the months at Manresa had been, they were never meant to be more than a preparation, albeit essential, for his journey to Jerusalem. So, in 1523, he went on from Manresa to Barcelona to take ship for Italy. His first stop was Rome, where at Eastertide he received with others a papal blessing on his pilgrimage. By a quirk of history the reigning Pope was the Dutchman Adrian VI, who died a few months later, after a pontificate of rather more than a year, and was to be the last non-Italian Pope for more than 450 years. From Rome Ignatius made his way on foot to Venice, where after much difficulty he found a place on a ship bound for Palestine by way of Cyprus.

He arrived at Jaffa on 25 August 1523 and went on two or three days later to Jerusalem, where he remained for three weeks. Like

St Francis before him, Ignatius wanted to stay on in Palestine, but
it was the Franciscans, official guardians of the holy places, who
refused him permission because their situation as Christian
representatives with the Turkish ruling authorities was always
precarious and they could not risk making exceptions which might
cause general trouble. So, on 23 September, he had to obey orders
and embark once more. It is clearly impossible for any Christian
to see the actual places in which Christ lived and taught and died
as mere tourist sights, and in the sixteenth century pilgrimage was
a much more popular devotion than it is now, but even in Ignatius'
bald account of his brief stay one can see extraordinarily direct
response to the concrete evidence of Christ's presence. He relates,
for instance, how, when he knew it was not God's will for him to
remain in Palestine, he stole out at night at considerable risk to
have another look at Mount Olivet. Thence, according to tradition, Christ ascended into heaven, leaving footprints still shown
to pilgrims fifteen hundred years later. Having bribed the guards,
Ignatius was able to inspect the place again, but having then gone
on to Bethphage, could not remember the respective angles of the
right and left feet, so he once more bribed the guards (with a pair
of scissors, his last possession) to satisfy himself on this point. A
Syrian Christian official met him coming down the mountainside
and escorted him none too gently to a monastery, but 'he felt
great consolation from Our Lord, and it seemed to him that he
saw Christ over him continually'.[2]

The significance of this apparently trivial incident is reflected in
the *Exercises*, an essential feature of which is to recreate in the
mind's eye, and indeed the other senses too, Christ's actual earthly
life, and Mount Olivet, with its unique (if questionable) imprint
of Christ's last moments on earth played an obviously important
part in Ignatius' own reconstruction of the life of Christ. As for
the abandonment of his hopes for remaining in Palestine, this
exemplifies the obedience to legitimate authority which henceforth
became an essential part of his life and teaching, and eventually
of his order. He had learned that true spiritual peace and the
discernment of spirits invariably involve self-denial in a human
sense, and that the acceptance of God's will is more often the
result of simple obedience to others than of following the secret
lure of inner voices. The problem, of course, is that the state of
uncertainty in which he, or anyone else, so often finds himself can
seldom be resolved by obedience because a major part of the
problem is finding someone to obey.

The next stage in his physical itinerary was at least clear, even if it was arduous. Having to leave Palestine he had no choice but to take ship again for Italy, and thus, after many months, came back to Venice. He no longer thought of retiring to a monastery, but after much pondering decided 'to study for some time so that he would be able to help souls', and to this end started off for Barcelona. In February or March 1524 he arrived there to continue a pilgrimage which had as yet no definite goal in time or place. The idea of helping souls was vague enough, but it must have been nourished and to some extent clarified by the growing number of contacts he had made since setting out from Loyola two years earlier. It certainly included the charitable acts of which the autobiography records a sample, but in the context it can only refer to passing on a message, or experience of Christ, with which he felt himself entrusted.

The pertinacity with which this now very mature student applied himself to study is all the more remarkable for the fact that he neither had in mind a specific career nor was attracted to intellectual pursuits for their own sake. It must be remembered, too, that having been born a Basque, Ignatius had already had to learn Spanish as a second language and now, aged thirty-three or so, he set himself to acquire Latin, beginning with lessons in elementary grammar. He stayed in Barcelona about two years, elaborating his *Exercises* all the time and attracting a few men and women as he expounded them. At the same time he read and decisively rejected Erasmus' enormously influential *Enchiridion*, with its anti-ritualistic emphasis on personal piety, moral rectitude, scripture reading and what has been called 'low tension Christianity'. Neither the cerebral coolness of Erasmus nor the somewhat quietistic and emotional style of the so-called *alumbrados* (enlightened ones: devout men and women who met in small informal groups and were, rightly or wrongly, suspected of heresy by the Inquisition) appealed to Ignatius, but in the religious climate of sixteenth-century Spain the defenders of orthodoxy were not inclined to look for nice distinctions among those who seemed to be different, and any nonconformist behaviour was likely to be put under the heading of the more familiar deviations.

In March 1526 Ignatius' Latin was adequate for him to move on to higher education, first at the University of Alcalá. He went on teaching the *Exercises* to all and sundry, together with one or two followers, and not surprisingly these raggedly dressed laymen were denounced as *alumbrados*. After six weeks in gaol they were cleared of the charge, but released on condition that they gave up their distinctive costume (rough clothes of the same colour) and taught no more until they had studied for three more years.

Eighteen months at Alcalá were followed by a shorter stay in Salamanca, where he was again imprisoned for unauthorized teaching. This time he had imprudently (later developments of Jesuit casuistry add a special irony) distinguished mortal and venial sins, and was told on release that he must study four more years before daring to teach moral theology again, although he can scarcely have realized that such elementary instruction could be dignified with the name of theology at all. Some ten years after Luther's revolt the Spanish authorities can hardly be blamed for their caution, and Ignatius by his age, always ragged appearance, and originality of style was too unusual to be encouraged. After a few weeks with old friends in Barcelona he once more set off on foot, knowing no French, through a land continually at war with his own, until in February 1528 he reached Paris.

He began by following the course at the Collège de Montaigu, where Erasmus had hated every minute of his student days thirty years before and where the young Calvin had been a member until the week before Ignatius' arrival. Another Parisian student, this time of Ignatius' own age, whom he could have met, was the irregular Benedictine, ex-Franciscan, François Rabelais. It is doubtful whether they would have found each other sympathetic. Paris had always been an international rather than a French university, and Ignatius was clearly right to aim at a degree which would be recognized everywhere and would incontrovertibly qualify him to teach, though by no means all subjects. After a year at Montaigu he migrated in 1529 to Sainte-Barbe, a few yards up the road, where he first met his fellow Basque Francis Xavier. By the end of 1532, an old man by the standards of the day, he graduated BA, finally proceeding to MA in 1534. Thus the ten gruelling years of study had at last produced their result, in Ignatius' own intellectual training and development and in a formal qualification. Besides the handicap of age (compare him with Calvin, a graduate at twenty), Ignatius had to beg his way through the student years, travelling to Flanders and even to London (1531) in the vacations to seek alms. After the MA he actually registered with the Dominicans to go on to read theology, but, as was then common, abandoned the course after a month or two. His studies were over and the next stage of his pilgrimage called him. From now on the story of Ignatius is part of the story of the Jesuits.

At Barcelona, Alcalá and Salamanca Ignatius had had what may loosely be called followers, but in Paris, perhaps just because he stayed there longer, a group formed round him which became the nucleus of his new order. The relationship with these six men was closer than previous associations, their aims were more precisely defined, and for the first time since his initial conversion Ignatius saw the pilgrimage as a joint enterprise. By mid-1534 each of the six had gone through the *Exercises* in turn, they had become accustomed to worshipping together and they took a momentous decision. On 15 August they all went up to the little chapel of the Martyrs (no longer extant) on the hill of that name (Montmartre) overlooking Paris. Pierre Favre, the only priest among them, celebrated mass and they all took vows of poverty, chastity and a pilgrimage to Jerusalem if possible, with the aim of settling there as missionaries. Should they be prevented from going to Jerusalem within a year of arriving in Venice (that is, by 1537), they would submit themselves to the Pope for whatever service he chose to assign them. This collective undertaking marks the effective, though not the official, beginning of the Society of Jesus.

Meanwhile Ignatius' health was causing grave concern (we now know that he suffered from biliary calculus) and for this and other reasons it was decided that he should go back to his homeland, there to rest and recuperate, and that they would all meet in Venice to wait for a boat. In March 1535 he duly arrived near Loyola (for family reasons he did not stay at the castle) and left the following November, never to see Spain again. Going on foot as usual he crossed Italy to Venice, and there, in early 1537, the original band of six with three new recruits at last assembled, their respective business done, to pursue their plan. Ignatius and his friends went on teaching, but he and most of the others earned their living during this waiting time by acting as hospital orderlies.

In March the others (not Ignatius) went to Rome to seek the usual papal authorization for their intended pilgrimage. Paul III willingly gave it, but in the prevailing political situation doubted whether they would get to Jerusalem. They then returned to Venice, and on 24 June 1537 Ignatius and five others were ordained priest (he was then forty-six, some thirteen years older than the next oldest). When it became clear that no boat would leave that year for Palestine, they agreed that the second part of their vow (submission to the Pope) now came into force, and the little band dispersed for a time, Ignatius going to Vicenza. It is worth reflecting that though prevented from going to Jerusalem, one of the band, Francis Xavier, would within four years be on his way to India, and eventually China and Japan, to inaugurate the Jesuit missionary record. It is also significant that Ignatius was never able to repeat his direct experience of the Holy Land nor share it with his co-founders.

In November they joined together again and journeyed to Rome. Not far from the city Ignatius had another critical mystical experience at a place called La Storta,[3] in which he saw that it was granted to him 'to serve Christ in a special way'. In the immediate context he took this to be a blessing not just on him but on his embryonic Society. At Christmas he at last said his first mass, in Santa Maria Maggiore, and, in the words of a Jesuit historian, he had recognized that God's service required him to make Rome his Jerusalem'.[4] Simply because a boat failed to sail, the second choice of Ignatius and his friends became the *raison d'être* of the Jesuits henceforth.

The rest of the story is quickly told. In September 1539 the Pope gave verbal approval to the new Society. They took a special vow of obedience to the Pope, were exempted from singing any choral office, and from any specific fasts or penances, and accepted an obligation to teach, in the first instance, children. A year later, on 27 September 1540, the Society was established formally by a papal bull, and limited to a maximum complement of sixty (there were ten of them at the time). By 1541 the new Constitutions had been finally worked out, and Ignatius was elected first General. Finally, in 1546, for local reasons, a college was opened at Gandia (near Valencia), and from then on schools for non-Jesuit students became a major activity of the Society and so remains. The great missionary activity in the Far East began under the aegis of the King of Portugal already in 1540, and soon contributed its quota of saints and martyrs to the growing prestige of the most powerful instrument of the Counter-Reformation. Ignatius himself remained in Rome, tirelessly supervising the world-wide activities of his Society despite indifferent health. His autobiography (up to the arrival in Rome in 1538) was dictated shortly before he died. On 31 July 1556 he was carried away so suddenly that he received neither communion nor unction. In the last fifteen years the original band of ten had increased to number a thousand.

These last years certainly included constant spiritual experiences, amounting to visions, of which some record can be found in Ignatius' fragmentary journal. We know, for example, that the perplexing problem of whether or not Jesuits should own property exercised Ignatius to such an extent that he sought a solution while saying mass over a number of days, eventually feeling that a negative answer had in some mystic way been revealed to him.

But the so-called pilgrim years, from the early days at Loyola recovering from his wound until the final arrival in Rome (1521–1538), constitute the process of conversion, followed by successive illuminations culminating in the specific call to found the Society as it still exists today.

To Jesuits themselves the causal link between the conversion of their founder, his *Exercises* and the highly distinctive nature of their own training and calling is no doubt self-evident, but this is hardly the case for an outsider. It must be said at once that the phenomenal expansion and power of the Jesuits throughout the seventeenth and eighteenth centuries, a power that all but led to their suppression, as much as their real power in modern times, can legitimately be attributed to their founder's spirit, but tends to obscure the issue as to what that spirit originally was. One comes back always to the *Exercises*, conceived at Manresa and continually revised until they reached their first (Latin) published form in 1548, being corrected in the original Spanish even after that by Ignatius.

Like so many, if not all, of the converts discussed in this book, Ignatius had the problems of communicating a deeply private spiritual experience, or series of experiences, in language such that others in the future might come to something like the same goal by paths less private and more intellectually accessible. If on the one hand this explains the uninviting style, the superficially dry schematization of the *Exercises*, it explains on the other hand the extraordinary and lasting effect they have had on countless Jesuits and others who have been taken through them, for there, veiled by frankly inadequate language, is the trace of what was experienced at a specific time, in a specific place, with a specific result, by the man Ignatius.

The *Spiritual Exercises* 'whereby to conquer oneself and order one's life without being influenced in one's decision by any inordinate affection' are devised to enable the exercitant to make an 'election', that is, to commit himself to a way of life in God's service. Ignatius distinguishes three 'times' of election, the first from above, when all is filled with radiance by a kind of revelation, the third from rational choice; but the second, of which he is the particular exponent, entails knowledge through consolation and aridity, above all through meditation on Christ's earthly life. The significance of the journey to Jerusalem, actual in Ignatius' own case, given highest priority though frustrated in the case of his first followers, at once becomes obvious. From the first, Ignatius was conscious of the 'struggle of spirits' in his own self and in the

whole of creation, and the typically Jesuit concept of the discernment of spirits represents his practical solution to a perennial
problem, and one to which the Reformation had given new
urgency. Equally his long sick-bed meditations at Loyola on
Christ's earthly life, inspired by Ludolph's book, gave him a yardstick to which the *Exercises* constantly refer. The Jesuit Hugo
Rahner shows how these early notions developed into the two
fundamental meditations of the *Exercises*, the 'call of the King'
and 'the two standards', and these in turn became intimately
bound up with ideas of the church. He writes: 'Ignatius [at Man-
resa] discovered the connection between his own spiritual battle
and the church, which itself is the field on which the visible Christ
wages war against the evil spirit.'[5]

The four 'weeks' of the *Exercises*, though divided into 'days',
do not correspond to any fixed period of time but mark successive
phases in the spiritual development of the exercitant, clearly
deriving from Ignatius' own experience. The self-examination and
meditation on hell of the first week give some idea of the violence
of Ignatius' inner struggle to overcome self. The 'call of the King'
and 'the two standards' of the second week show the soul's
recognition of its duty to serve Christ as sovereign lord of all
creation, but also an awareness that the enemy, Lucifer, is constantly waging war beneath the standard of sin. One of the exercises actually requires a mental picture of two great armies drawn
up by Jerusalem and Babylon respectively, seen as real cities.
Ignatius' own experience as a soldier and his early interest in
romances of chivalry evidently play some part in the feudal and
military framework of these images, but the spirit of crusade was
far from extinguished at a time when the Turkish threat was all
too real and such martial imagery was commonplace. After the
tumult and shouting, the third week is devoted to meditations on
the passion and the fourth to the resurrection and a contemplation
on love, consolidating the foregoing with exercises in joy.

A vital element is that concerned with the discernment of spirits
and with the role of the church. The often wild excesses of fasting
and despair, the strange visions and tormenting scruples of the
early months at Manresa, represent confusion, while the Cardoner
experience introduces order and stability. The dangers of subjectivity and self-delusion in powerful spiritual experiences are always
acute, and the claims of Luther, not to mention the sectarians,
Anabaptists and the like, were to add point to the need for some
objective control as the century wore on.

Ignatius throughout his life submitted himself to others: to the

Franciscan provincial at Jerusalem; to his confessor at Manresa; to the authorities, ecclesiastical and academic, at Alcalá, Salamanca and Paris; finally and above all to the Pope. Furthermore, he drew up, as spiritual writers had done before him, lists of the effects, spiritual, mental and even physical, of good and bad spirits respectively so that some objective criteria could be applied to any doubtful experience. Thus no spiritual experience, however overwhelming, risked getting out of control; no follower of Ignatius, however bewildered, was left without a guide. It is, of course, true that the external discipline is military in its rigour, and as the Society grew, its members soon came to resemble an army in their blind obedience to orders, but it is probably misleading to see in this unmistakably military organization any special predilection on Ignatius' part. Indeed the ragged group he assembled round him looked much more like modern guerillas than guardsmen. The point is, rather, that Ignatius' vision of Christ, his realization of the incessant threat of ambush by selfish forces masquerading as divine inspiration, and, later, the disruption of the church by appeals to individual conscience and personal interpretation of scripture, all these things impelled him from the start to set himself under orders. Hugo Rahner writes: 'The authenticity of any spiritual movement has become measurable against the life of Christ on earth', and he adds that Ignatius' personal obedience in Jerusalem meant that 'the ideal of performing some concrete task within the hierarchical church was thenceforth to take clearer shape in his mind'.[6] Finally, he writes, Ignatius had 'the mystical conviction, ever since Manresa, that the presence of the spirit is bodied forth in Christ. And because of this there could for Ignatius be ultimately no contradiction between Spirit and church, between love and letter.'[7] It is precisely for that reason that he laid down quite explicitly that all the targets of reformers from Erasmus onwards, like pilgrimage, votive candles and so on, in themselves indifferent, should be unquestioningly respected as expressions of the church's authority. Obedience and self-abasement, not the future tactics required by the Counter-Reformation, originally inspired this positive defence, rather than passive acceptance of the hierarchical church. This is what Ignatius learned at Manresa, as part of his conversion, and if the Popes were glad to use the weapon of Jesuit obedience presented to them, it was Ignatius who had forged it for himself, not they.

4

BLAISE PASCAL

The most important single fact about Pascal is that he was intellectually a genius. It was as such that he was treated from boyhood, as such that he was respected by mathematicians and scientists throughout Europe during his short life. Perhaps the second most important thing about him is that he was lonely, and suffered such poor health that he could not afford to be alone without care. He was a person of astonishing versatility, practical as well as theoretical, and enormous charm in company and on paper. The work best known in his lifetime was published anonymously, his authorship not at all widely known; his greatest work was posthumous, and appeared in distorted form, with a half-hearted introduction, but three hundred years later still sells thousands of copies a year, though it remains insolubly fragmentary. Very few of his contemporaries would recognize Pascal from the reputation he enjoys today; very few of us would suspect that the author of the *Pensées* was the same M. Pascal whom the general public of his own day knew as a transport pioneer, the salons as a witty conversationalist and the learned world as an internationally respected scientist. He was brilliant, and he was proud; he was lonely, and he was insecure. The two aspects cannot be separated, but they can only be reconciled in the context of his conversion.

The loneliness came first. Pascal was born in 1623, and lost his mother only three years later. His father never remarried, and Blaise, with his elder sister Gilberte and younger sister Jacqueline, grew up in a family which, however close and affectionate, was incomplete. The boy never went to school, but was educated by his father. He thus escaped the roughness of boys of his own age, but also their companionship. Intellectually his standards were set not by fellow pupils or even teachers, but by his father's friends and frequent visitors from among the leading mathematicians of France. To hold his own with men like Mersenne, Fermat and Roberval, Blaise had to be a prodigy, and he was. His sense of identity must from an early age have been centred on his intellectual distinction. As for emotional development, he depended heavily on his sisters, especially Jacqueline, and after Gilberte married in 1641 her children eventually came as close as anyone could to enjoying his protective affection. As a son he expected preferential treatment, and such evidence as we have suggests that he was spoilt by his sisters and his father. Certainly he depended on them more than they on him.

Information about Pascal's religious upbringing and beliefs does not go beyond the conventional record of where the family worshipped and which ceremonies of baptism and the like he attended, but in 1646 an event occurred which enables us to guess more accurately what had been the situation up till then. The family had by now left Paris for Rouen, where Pascal's father held a post in government service. As a result of a fall, Etienne Pascal made the acquaintance of two brothers who were, among other things, amateur bonesetters. Their talents extended, however, beyond physical repair and through them the Pascal family for the first time made direct contact with the very distinctive form of spirituality taught by Saint-Cyran and practised by those who came to be called Jansenists.

Saint-Cyran had for years been the friend and correspondent of Cornelius Jansen, who became Bishop of Ypres and died (1638) shortly before publication of his weighty tome on St Augustine, the *Augustinus* (1640). Saint-Cyran had become spiritual director of the originally Cistercian and then autonomous nuns at Port-Royal (they had houses both in Paris and near Versailles, and the latter was occupied at different times by male solitaries and nuns, while sympathizers of both sexes lived nearby). He had fallen foul of Richelieu on a political issue, spent some five years in prison and was released only to die a few months later in 1643. His successor was the professional theologian Antoine Arnauld, two of whose sisters became abbesses of Port-Royal.

At this stage Saint-Cyran's followers were not yet a party, but they represented a tendency in the Catholic church not easily compatible with that of certain other groups, especially the Jesuits. What may conveniently, and perhaps inaccurately, be called Jansenism was a deliberate attempt to go back to the Fathers and the

Bible in a reaction against the essentially man-centred theology
and practice of the Counter-Reformation. There was no question
of adopting Protestant positions; on the contrary, Saint-Cyran and
Jansen had seen in rigorism and orthodoxy, based on the most
respected authorities, the best way to counteract Protestantism
without betraying Christ as, they thought, the Jesuits and their
laxist allies were doing. Theologically their most characteristic
doctrine concerned grace, which they believed to be God's free
gift and the only way to salvation, as against the works theology
of Molina, espoused by the Jesuits. Institutionally they were
implacably opposed to schism, whatever the grounds, and were in
fact more closely identified with the parochial and hierarchical
system than were the largely autonomous Jesuits. Spiritually they
taught a rejection of worldly values, in extreme cases leading to
the kind of solitary life without vows of the gentlemen (*'ces Mes-
sieurs'*) of Port-Royal, but more usually to a 'being in the world
without being of it' mentality. They strongly emphasized discipline, in the first instance submission to a director, to avoid temptations of subjectivism, and also sacramental discipline, which was
taken so seriously that on occasions Jansenists would abstain from
communion as a penance until their spiritual disposition became
healthy again. Their general bent was for simplicity, personal and
not mechanical devotion, a directly christocentric piety with less
attention paid to invocation of saints than was usual at the time,
and a strong emphasis on direct works of charity for the poor,
education for children, serious living free from extravagance and
frivolity. In a word, Christianity became a whole way of life, going
far beyond dogma and external acts of piety.

Under the guidance of a neighbouring curé the Pascal family
threw themselves enthusiastically into this new spiritual way, and,
when they returned to live in Paris next year, among the contacts
they made were some with the man and women of the Port-Royal
communities. Jacqueline, an impulsive, sensitive girl, wanted to
join the nuns, but her father vetoed such a move, and, since
without his financial support it would have been difficult, she
deferred to his objections. Blaise seems to have been affected
rather more cerebrally, and tried to support his faith with reasons
and words, but one can only assess the quality of his religious
convictions and feelings from the kind of life he led and the
account of his second conversion some years later.

He frequented aristocratic salons, met Descartes twice (but not
in a salon, because he was bedridden at the time), accompanied
his friend the Duc de Roannez to Poitou, where he was involved

in an ambitious enterprise for reclaiming marshland, and met well-known society figures, like Méré, the arbiter of elegance, and Miton, a prominent gambler. The Roannez, especially the Duc's sister Charlotte, were anything but frivolous, and for a time Charlotte too vainly tried to become a nun, but during this so-called worldly period Pascal cannot be said to have turned his back very decisively on worldly values. He was, it is true, still very young, the social and intellectual life of Paris must have been very exciting after that of Rouen, and his public controversy with the Jesuit Scholastic, Père Noël, over the vacuum brought him fame as well as fun, particularly on the successful completion of the experiments organized on the Puy-de-Dôme and elsewhere. The tone of his letters to Noël shows a not unpleasant youthful arrogance. He took legitimate pride in upsetting physical theories hallowed by antiquity, but it was unmistakably pride at his own cleverness, and in the context of his religion he was neither practising humility nor renouncing worldly values, though few would think any the worse of him for that. The point is that at a recorded moment in his life he thought the worse of himself.

In 1651 Pascal's father died, and Blaise wrote a remarkable letter to Gilberte about death. The explicitly Augustinian tone (and quotations) leaves very little room for doubt as to his convictions at the time. He emphasizes the danger of becoming attached to creatures, dismisses Seneca and Socrates (typical of Stoic models) as useless guides to a Christian death, and works up to an Augustinian conclusion about the two loves, of God and self, both innocent before the Fall, but thereafter incompatible. It is not a gentle message, but in its uncompromising reminder of God's total demands on man it may have proved a real comfort to his sister. At the same time there is no reason to doubt that Pascal himself gave not only intellectual but also emotional assent to the austere doctrines presented in this letter. He missed his father in a normal human way, but his faith made him see the loss as his father's gain.

The tone of equanimity need not be questioned, but the following three years were to expose his faith to a test which, in retrospect, Pascal seems to have found too much for him. The crucial factor was, from all the evidence, Jacqueline's entry into Port-Royal, made possible by her father's death, but at the same time depriving Blaise yet again of a reassuring presence. There was trouble, even animosity, over the financial arrangements, which could not be settled honourably for some time; there were practical problems about his living alone in precarious health, and perhaps Jacqueline's spiritual certainty forced him to ask himself uncomfortable and intimate questions. The psychology of bereavement is a complex matter, especially in such a case as Pascal's, who had never known a mother, and in rapid succession now saw himself deprived of father and sister. At the very least he was confused, lonely, probably resentful and self-pitying. It is likely that he felt a call, either inwardly or through his sister, to make some sacrifice comparable with hers; if he did, he certainly resisted it.

The events of the three years following his father's death in 1651 are not very informative in themselves: work on various mathematical problems; correspondence with Fermat, a leading mathematician; legal and financial matters, including the acquisition in 1654 of a house (in what is now the rue Monsieur-le-Prince); continued frequentation of salons and of his friend Roannez. By no standards could such activities be regarded as wicked, but by those of Pascal (and of Gilberte in her biography of her brother) they were seen as worldly. The time had come for a final decision.

On the night of 23 November 1634 Pascal had an experience of which a precise, but secret, record survives. He copied out twice, on parchment and on paper, the extraordinary account known as the *Memorial* and kept the two scraps sewn into the lining of his clothes, where they were accidentally discovered after his death. It is fair to ask what one could guess of the experience, whether one could even guess that one had occurred, if the only evidence remaining were that of Pascal's written work and the comments of those who knew him best. On the face of it what happened to him is reflected in a far more active involvement with Port-Royal, illustrated by the (reconstructed) *Entretien avec M. de Sacy* (1655), the *Lettres Provinciales* (1656–7) and, above all, the unfinished *Apologie*, of which the extent fragments constitute the *Pensées* (1657–62). To this one could add contributions to the Jansenist cause, like the *Ecrits sur la Grâce* and private papers, like the meditation *Mystère de Jésus*. Just where the international competition on the problem of the cycloid (to which Christopher Wren and Christiaan Huyghens contributed) comes in is a nice point, but the *carosses à 5 sous* (a public coach service), the profits of which were intended for the poor of Blois, and the Poitevin land reclamation, for the benefit of local farmers rather than the capitalist entrepreneurs, are less incongruous. All in all it can be seen that the last seven years of Pascal's life were devoted mainly to specifically Christian occupations, and only incapacitating illness limited this devotion. Clearly something had crystallized in his heart and mind, but only the *Memorial* can explain just what.

The text is so important that is must be given in full (the italicized phrases were originally written in Latin):

> Fire
> 'God of Abraham, God of Isaac, God of Jacob', not of philosophers and scholars.
> Certainty, certainty, heartfelt joy, peace.
> God of Jesus Christ.
> God of Jesus Christ.
> *My God and your God.*
> The world forgotten, and everything except God.
> He can only be found by the ways taught in the Gospels.
> Greatness of the human soul.
> 'O righteous Father, the world had not known thee, but I have known thee.'
> Joy, joy, joy, tears of joy.
> I have cut myself off from him.
> *They have forsaken me, the fountain of living waters.*
> 'My God, wilt thou forsake me?'
> Let me not be cut off from him for ever!
> 'And this is life eternal, that they might know thee, the only true
> God, and Jesus Christ whom thou hast sent.'
> Jesus Christ.
> Jesus Christ.
> I have cut myself off from him, shunned him, denied him, crucified him.
> Let me never be cut off from him!
> He can only be kept by the ways taught in the Gospel.
> Sweet and total renunciation.
> Total submission to Jesus Christ and my director.
> Everlasting joy in return for one day's effort on earth,
> *I will not forget thy word.* Amen. *(913)*

As with most of Pascal's writing, this record shows a strikingly antithetical pattern. On the one side is the true God he has found, the God of the Old and of the New Testaments, the person Jesus; on the other one are the false gods, philosophy, science, worldliness. From the march of the argument (because it may properly be called a spiritual argument) all the words of separation in the second part are to be linked with the choice of these false gods over the gospel truth in the first part. The hinge is the fourfold repetition of the keyword 'joy'. But if joy is associated with 'certainty, peace, sweet and total renunciation' and, above all, 'terms', the implied antithesis can hardly be missed. In the *Pensées* Pascal writes of the human condition without God as being 'inconstancy, boredom, anxiety' (*24*), which we seek to alleviate by diversions of all sorts. In Augustinian terms we suffer from putting our finite, flawed selves at the centre where God should be, thereby ensuring frustration and unhappiness. Pascal had gone his own way; behind all the appearances of piety, so applauded by Gilberte, behind the words and even the intellectual assent, he had witheld the best part of himself. He had not so much failed to love God as rejected God's love for him.

There is some evidence (from handwriting) that the last three phrases may have been added later, at the end of his life, though this is not at all certain, but whether they express an intention or a conclusion they describe what he did, and with what effect. He will not just privately submit to Christ, but also openly to his director who, rather than Pascal himself, will prescribe the rule of life, and this rule, this 'one day's effort on earth', is all that is demanded of him as the price of eternal joy. His effort alone would be of no effect, but the call to salvation, which we must take the *Memorial* to record, was at the same time a call to specific action. He may probably add that such action (that is, a Christian life of self-denial under obedience) is that part of salvation which, so to speak, is offered in advance, because living in union with Christ in this life is the nearest mortal man can come to the beatific vision hereafter.

The experience of the November night was not in any usual sense of the word a vision. It is doubtful whether it can even be called mystical, but it seems rather to have been a meditation and a dialogue, in which Pascal is responding to specific statements (probably verbal) of an interior voice, that of God. The experience involved a call, to which Pascal gave his assent; an admission of guilt, for which he recognizes that he has been forgiven; and a declaration of love, given and received. The immediate result was joy, liberation from the bonds of self, and wholeness, an integration of his life with God's will and his fellow Christians. Pride and loneliness were thus conquered together.

The questions posed by the *Memorial* are endless: how far does the second conversion compel reassessment of the first (1647)? How long had Pascal felt separated from God? And which specific manifestations of sin caused his feelings of alienation? The durability of this second conversion does not seem to be in doubt;

Pascal had found his way and followed it. Although any true conversion involves some renunciation of the world, the physical and social withdrawal would not in itself seem adequately to distinguish Pascal's subsequent from his previous conduct. The only framework within which to judge what had happened to him is that of the two Augustinian loves. If the promise of the *Memorial* was kept as we have every reason to believe, it was not so much, or at all, in change of conduct as in change of heart. Writers on monastic life often stress the danger of practising austerity for reasons of spiritual pride, and Pascal's hairshirt and spiked belt (worn secretly and discovered only at his death) are not even *prima facie* evidence of penitential humility. After November 1654 he was animated in all he did by the love of God and of his neighbour. His life made sense, Christian sense, where before it has been correct, but out of focus.

This discussion of Pascal's development has so far been in terms of the Augustinian antithesis, an either-or, but in his own terms there is another way of looking at the change of heart: with reference to the theory of orders. The word 'heart' is of crucial importance in that context and involves a transposition of all the values in his life from one order to another. While Pascal would probably always describe conversion in this way, it is unlikely that anyone else, unless closely influenced by his thought, would do so, and to that extent the description of what happened, the habit of mind behind the description, may even have influenced Pascal's reactions.

The first explicit statement of the theory of orders comes in the strictly scientific context of the controversy over the vacuum, and is seen most clearly in the unfinished *Preface* to the *Traité du Vide*. The Jesuit, Père Noël, and other traditionalists had challenged Pascal's presumption in setting himself up against the authority of the ancients (ultimately Aristotle). Pascal replied by dividing all knowledge into three categories or orders: that which came through the senses, such as the empirical data underlying his theory of the vacuum; that which came through the intellect, such as logic or the principles of mathematics; and that which came from submission to authority, pre-eminently the revealed truths of religion. He accused his opponents of innovating in religion by invoking rational and human criteria, while suppressing scientific progress with illegitimate appeals to the authority of obsolete ancients. So far his distinction between the orders is an intellectual one, appropriate to his polemical purpose.

Some six years later, in the eighteenth *Provincial Letter*, (1657), a very similar pattern appears as he challenges the Jesuit Annat to produce hard evidence in the form of page references to the presence of any, or all, of the incriminated *Five Propositions* in the *Augustinus*, on which the charge of heresy was based. Pascal and the Jansenists did not question the Pope's right to censure doctrine, and to require the faithful to subscribe to such censure. He asks his opponent the question: 'How do we learn the truth about facts?', and answers: 'From our eyes, which are the rightful judge of fact, as reason is of natural and intelligible things, and faith of things supernatural and revealed.'[1] The context is again polemical, and the distinction intellectual, because intended to convince the reader (and perhaps even the Jesuit). Faith here could equally well mean obedient acceptance of the church's teaching as personal conviction, and this formulation is therefore consistent both with the earlier one and with 'submission to my director'.

The fullest development of this idea of three orders of know-ledge comes in the *Pensées* and must have been formulated by Pascal at about the same time as the later *Provincial Letters*. It is hard to say exactly how or when Pascal began to apply the cer-tainty of his conversion experience to the triple pattern of human knowledge, but the complete fusion of the two produced one of his most characteristic ideas. A magnificent fragment (*308*) sets out this revised pattern in an existential, not an epistemological way. 'Kings, rich men, captains . . . are all great in a carnal sense' and an infinite distance separates their greatness from that of Archimedes, great in mind, but 'Jesus without wealth or any outward shows of knowledge has his own order of holiness'. The fragment concludes: 'Out of all bodies together we could not succeed in creating one little thought. It is impossible, and of a different order. Out of all bodies and minds we could not extract one impulse of true charity. It is impossible, and of a different supernatural order.' Here holiness and charity are near synonyms.

Another key fragment takes us back to epistemology: 'We know the truth not only through our reason but also through our heart. It is through the latter that we know first principles . . . like space, time, motion, number . . . and it is on such knowledge, coming from the heart and instinct, that reason has to depend and base all its argument.' Rather unexpectedly, this passage concludes on an unmistakably personal note: 'Those to whom God has given religious faith by moving their hearts are very fortunate, and feel quite legitimately convinced, but to those who do not have it, we can only give such faith through reasoning, until God gives it by

moving their heart, without which faith is only human and useless
for salvation' (*110*). As a commentary on the November night
those last phrases are most illuminating. Add a briefer fragment
(*172*) and the process is even clearer: 'The way of God, who
disposes all things with gentleness, is to instil religion into our
minds with reasoned arguments and into our hearts with grace.'

A fragment actually entitled 'order' (*298*) goes even further:

> The heart has its order, the mind has its own, which uses
> principles and demonstrations. The heart has a different one.
> We do not prove that we ought to be loved by setting out in
> order the causes of love, that would be absurd.
>
> Jesus Christ and St Paul possess the order of charity, not of
> the mind, for they wished to humble, not to teach.
>
> The same with St Augustine. This order consists mainly in
> digressions upon each point which relates to the end, so that
> this [end] shall be kept always in sight.

Heart and charity go together, and the last sentence is very
apposite to Pascal's own method in the *Pensées*.

One of the most famous of all the *Pensées* is (*423*): 'The heart
has its reasons of which reason knows nothing', and it is immediately followed by one of equal importance but less fame (*424*);
'It is the heart which perceives God and not the reason. That is
what faith is: God perceived by the heart, not the reason.'

Holiness, charity, heart, grace, faith, all these words belong to
the same order, and it is neither the order of body, materialism,
nor mind, intellectualism. This is the crux; Pascal's conversion
had let him see God in Christ, and all things through Christ. Pride
had estranged and blinded him, pride had made him lonely by
cutting him off from the acceptance of God's love, and thus from
any truly unselfish relationship with others. Once he had accepted
love he could give it; once his heart had found the truth he could
pass it on to others in the form of reasoned arguments. Even this
was not all, and in his attitude to the poor, the humble and the
simple he showed a real sense of practical solidarity. He took a
poor family into his home during his last illness, he tried to arrange
for an advance of his share of the *carosses* so that the poor of
Blois should not have to wait for their needed relief, and his sister
records other examples of practical caring. His daily life was one
of monastic austerity, even when he was terminally ill; he served
God and his neighbour with his body and his goods. But more
important still in his recognition of the truth that the élite in this
world, defined by intellectual or material standards, may and do

find it harder to come to God than the simple. The half-dozen fragments of the final section (*Conclusion*) show beyond all doubt what conversion meant to Pascal.

> What a long way it is between knowing God and loving him!
> (*377*)

> True conversion consists in self-annihilation . . . in knowing that there is an irreconcilable opposition between God and us, and that without a mediator there can be no exchange. (*378*)

> Do not be astonished to see simple people believing without argument. God makes them love him and hate themselves.
> (*380*)

> Those whom we see to be Christians without knowledge of the prophecies and proofs are no less sound judges than those who possess such knowledge. They judge with their hearts as others judge with their minds. (*381*)

Pascal the genius did not betray intellect, as some of his intellectual critics maintain; he brought it back where it belonged. He did not seek salvation in an absolute Franciscan poverty, but shared his worldly goods with others. He denied not reason, but pride in reason; he abandoned the loneliness of independence for the fellowship of charity. He accepted the imperative of Christ's love for all men and suddenly felt free to love in return. Expressed in these terms, Pascal's conversion is a fulfilment, not a denial – grace always fulfils nature – and by enabling him to break out of the claustrophobic and illusory self-sufficiency of his earlier way of life helped him to find himself more fully than ever before.

5

ARMAND-JEAN DE RANCÉ

Armand-Jean Bouthillier de Rancé was born in 1626, that is, three years after Pascal, underwent a conversion in 1657, at exactly the same age as Pascal, but made his final decision to become a monk only five or six years later, in 1662 or 1663, at just the time of Pascal's death. From then until his death in 1700 he wrote a vast number of letters, of which some two thousand have survived in one form or another, and, from 1683, began to publish on monastic and spiritual subjects a number of books which, despite such a very late start, easily exceeds the total volume of all that Pascal left both in print and manuscript. It is, of course, not for his books, or even his letters, that he is known today, but for his abbey of la Trappe, which he reformed, and virtually refounded, and from which the Trappists, or Cistercians of the Strict Observance, ultimately derive.

There is no record of the two men meeting, and Rancé never mentions Pascal by name (though he may be the subject of one or more cryptic allusions in letters), but it is certain that Rancé knew of Pascal, and highly probable that they met. The Oratorian Père de Saint-Pé knew Rancé well, and had been a close friend of the Pascal family in Rouen from about 1644, and M. Duhamel, with whom Rancé was intimate and who would have died at la Trappe if relatives had not come to fetch him away during his last illness, had actually been curé of Saint-Merri in Paris when Pascal and the Roannez lived in the parish. In addition, the salons and society they frequented before their respective conversions were so similar that they can hardly have avoided contact. They had the same Jansenist friends at Port-Royal and elsewhere, and it is only surprising that there is no mention among the many acknowledgements of books Rancé received from them of the *Pensées*. If illness had not cut short Pascal's life it is hardly to be doubted that he would have visited la Trappe like Arnauld, Nicole and other leading Jansenists, and it is tempting to compose the imaginary conversation with Rancé.

All these points of contact and similarity help to situate Rancé historically and, to some extent, spiritually, and they are by no means exhaustive. Yet, when all is said and done, it is the differences which make each one of us unique, and neither Pascal nor Rancé invites categorization. The chief obstacle to knowing and understanding Rancé is the legend, sedulously fostered in his lifetime by smaller men who hoped to claim friendship with a canonized saint once he was dead, perpetuated for his own glory by Chateaubriand,[1] and spitefully countered for many reasons from well before his death to the present day by those who, not unreasonably, resent exaggerated claims to sanctity made on behalf of such a controversial figure. It is at last possible to pierce the twin curtains of hagiography and hostility to reveal the man in something like his true shape.

Rancé's childhood was spent mainly in Paris, where his father filled various government posts, and near Tours, of which see his uncle became Archbishop and where, at Véretz, his father bought a splendid estate. The failing health of an elder brother, who died in 1637, brought about a change in the plans made for Armand. Originally destined for a career of arms as a Knight of Malta, he quite suddenly found himself switched to a career in the church. The family benefices intended for his brother were now allotted to him, and by 1638 his barely adolescent shoulders were weighed down under the burden of two titles of abbot and three of prior, all, of course, commendatory (that is, honorary and usually absentee), but no less lucrative for that. He managed to combine these offices with a canonry of Notre-Dame in Paris.

At the same time as his brother's death and his own preferment, Rancé saw one older sister go off to a convent and another to a husband, and then, in 1638, his mother suddenly died, leaving at least two daughters and a son all younger than Armand, as well as the adult children. Since there is no reliable information about his relations with his mother, all that can be safely affirmed is that such a loss at such an age is often critical for emotional development. One of these younger sisters, Louise-Isabelle, later (1647) became an Annonciade nun with the name of Marie-Louise and outlived him by some years. His letters to her show warmth and intimacy over a long period (1662–1697), and suggest that they had always been particularly close. Another known feminine influence in these early years was that of Marie Bouthillier, wife of Rancé's uncle Claude and mother of the minister Chavigny. He went to her for advice after his conversion, she superintended the education of his sister's children, and had a reputation for genuine practical piety. There was also his neighbour, the Duchesse de Montbazon (1612–57), whose beauty and marriage to a man forty-four years her senior gave her a certain reputation for amours which must have had some basis in fact. If the precise nature of her influence is hard to affirm, there can be no doubt that she played a critical part in his emotional development.

Like most boys of his rank, Rancé did not go to school, and even when he went to university attended at the Collège de Harcourt for only a year, taking the rest of his instruction from tutors. There is evidence that he was very gifted, and in 1652 he was placed first in his licence in theology (Bossuet was third). By then he had proceeded through the various minor orders to the priesthood (1651), and on losing his father (1650) found himself head of a wealthy and distinguished family. His uncle Victor, Archbishop of Tours, was keen to further his career, and seems to have envisaged making him coadjutor with eventual right of succession. He distinguished himself at the Clergy Assembly in 1655, was appointed chaplain to Gaston d'Orléans, the King's uncle, in 1656, and in 1657 was piqued to be rejected by Mazarin, no friend of his family, for the post of coadjutor to his uncle.

So far he was climbing, fairly rapidly, the rungs of the traditional ladder to ecclesiastical distinction, and combining this with vigorous social activity as a typical *abbé de cour* (society priest). He had numerous friends, mostly of his own, newly ennobled, class of senior official, some of them in orders, some pursuing a secular career. He obviously knew many women of high birth in the salons, because his later letters constantly allude to acquaintance in the world, but it is significant that his most scurrilous critics mention no name save that of Mme de Montbazon. His favourite pastime seems to have been horse riding, but he is mentioned by contemporary gossip writers as cutting something of a figure in the salons, especially in 1656–7 when smart society was enjoying the anonymous *Provincial Letters* as they appeared. As a theologian and an ecclesiastical politician he knew all about Jansenism as a doctrine and a party; as an habitué of certain salons he knew, or knew of, the leading Jansenist personalities. To that extent he was intellectually aware that his worldly conduct was in conformity with that of other society priests, pushed into the church by their families, but hardly with evangelical precept.

He liked and sought success, social and professional; he was headstrong and impulsive, a man of extremes; he had a gift and need for friendship, but it is quite impossible to say how far his clerical celibacy impeded his emotional growth. The main clue to the latter is an extraordinarily durable relationship with his former tutor, Jean Favier, who actually survived him by a year or two, and to whom he wrote regularly for more than fifty years. Without mother or father, Rancé needed approval and reassurance from an older person whom he could respect. It would be almost certainly wrong to say that Rancé was lonely as Pascal had been – he had too many distractions – but he was proud and he was emotionally vulnerable.

After his rebuff by Mazarin over the coadjutorship, Rancé left the Assembly and Paris and retired to Vérets. Suddenly deciding to visit his friends in Paris, he arrived at the house of Madam de Montbazon to find that arrangements for her funeral were proceeding: she had died of scarlet fever on 28 April 1657 and he had known nothing about it. If conversion can be dated from a sudden shock, this was unquestionably such a shock, and he never resumed his former way of life, though he still had a long way to go before he reached his still unknown goal.

He did not attend the funeral, but went straight back to Véretz. There the first person he consulted was Mère Louise Rogier, a woman with whom he seems to have been on close terms for some time, probably through his aunt, Mme Bouthillier, and his sister's children, who were being educated in the Visitation convent at Tours of which Mère Louise was several times superior. Ten years older than Rancé, Louise Rogier (1616–1707) had from 1637–40 been the mistress of Gaston d'Orléans, to whom she had borne a son. For no very clear reason she decided to leave the world, and was professed in 1644 at the convent where she spent the rest of her long life. About a hundred letters of Rancé to her survive, and in the beginning she is very clearly supporting him, though in the course of the years the roles became reversed. The choice of a woman with her history for confidant is hardly surprising; she had known and renounced the world to find peace in a cloister, and as a reformed sinner could be expected to understand his problem.

From now on perhaps the most striking feature of Rancé's long process of arriving at a decision is the very large number of people he consulted. At first he seems genuinely to have wanted to be

told what to do, and in the first six months submitted himself to
an Oratorian director (Mère Louise had close contacts with the
Oratory, and through her he began a lifelong association with
members of that congregation), spent a week or two at Port-Royal
with Arnauld d'Andilly (one of the vast Arnauld clan and a former
member of Gaston's entourage) and gone into gentlemanly retreat
at Véretz on a mildly austere diet, with some good books (mostly
Church Fathers) and a few pious friends for company. He had
halted in mid-career, but had not yet made a positive start in a
new direction. For one thing, the practical problem of divesting
himself of his benefices and family fortune could not be solved
overnight; for another, he was not yet sure which road to follow
now that he had forsaken all.

The process continued slowly but according to a discernible
plan. First he inspected his abbeys and priories to assess what was
needed, then he initiated the sluggish process of transfer to worthy
successors, not without difficulty deciding in the end to keep just
la Trappe for himself.

Rancé and all his family were profoundly loyal to the crown,
and nominal though his duties were, Rancé felt committed by his
post as chaplain to Gaston. Gaston's sudden death in 1660 at last
freed him, and his immediate, and typical, response, was to plan
a long journey to the Pyrenees to seek yet more advice, this time
from the saintly Bishop Pavillon of Alet. The Bishop, and his
episcopal neighbours at Comminges and Pamiers, seem to have
urged him to assume similar pastoral responsibility to their own,
but Rancé was reluctant to do so. It is at this stage, in 1660, that
we have the first record of Rancé's reaction to the suggestion that
he might become a monk, exchanging his commendatory status
for that of regular abbot or prior. A letter written in 1688 by
Gilbert de Choiseul, by then Bishop of Tournai but in 1660 still
at Comminges, describes Rancé's horror at the very idea that he
might become a *frocard* (a very disparaging term for monk).

By 1662 the financial and administrative details had almost been
cleared up, and in August Rancé went to supervise the reform of
the decaying abbey of la Trappe. As late as this he was still
intending to retire to his other remaining benefice, the Gram-
montine priory of Boulogne, near Chambord, but seeing how
much material and spiritual work was urgently required at la
Trappe, in September he went back to spend the winter there
rather than at Boulogne. A letter written later speaks of this as
the moment when he 'began to see clearly'. By April 1663 his
conversion had at last assumed formal and irrevocable shape; he

went through the necessary formalities and in June 1663 received the Cistercian habit at Perseigne, the monastery nearest la Trappe. A year later he was solemnly professed, and in July 1664 took over as regular abbot of la Trappe, where he was to spend the next thirty-six years.

Thus from initial shock to final decision fully six years elapsed, and it does not seem fanciful to regard that lonely winter 1662–3 spent at la Trappe as a second, definitive conversion. It is curious that throughout the period of six years he was in constant correspondence with Mère Louise, Andilly and others (these letters are the most reliable extant record of his development), but the crucial decision seems to have been taken when he was quite alone in the crumbling monastery of la Trappe, and he certainly did not choose to spend the winter there on the advice of anyone else. Choiseul reminded him in the spring of 1663 of his horrified rejection of precisely the course he had now chosen to adopt, and which even the Cistercian authorities viewed with misgiving. The seed had been planted in the Pyrenees and grew almost unnoticed to fruition.

Fortunately Rancé's voluminous correspondence leaves no room for doubt concerning his motives. His was a purely personal conversion, a way to settle his own accounts with God, and absolutely not a conscious, or deliberate, prelude to the amazing career that followed. Shortly after taking up his abbatial duties he wrote to Mère Louise in July 1664:[2]

> I have consecrated the rest of my days to a state which seemed to be most base and despicable [a confirmation of his *frocard* remark] and therefore most fitting for doing penance for my sins . . . I saw myself as a man condemned to hell by the number and gravity of his sins, and I thought at the same time that the only way to appease the wrath of God was to commit myself to a penance which will only finish when my life does.

Subsequent events prove that however dramatic these words may sound, not only did Rancé live them out, but overcame quite unforeseen obstacles in so doing. Originally, there can be no doubt, his need for penitence was entirely personal and private. His birth and upbringing made him almost automatically accept the rank and responsibility of abbot, but la Trappe was a poor, ruined and obscure house with less than a dozen monks, six of whom were on loan from Perseigne as a nucleus of reform. At some stage, early on in his conversion, responsibility for others, specifically leading the same life as he under his guidance, replaced

the desire for a purely solitary solution. From the start his personal
wealth and contacts enormously improved the fortunes of his
abbey, and this was clearly a right use of his talents. Others,
however, had other ideas, and he had not been a monk for much
more than a year, or abbot for more than a week or two, when
for the first time in his life he was confronted with the demands
of the vow of obedience.

However he may have viewed his future, his superiors in the
reforming party of the Cistercian order were overjoyed at having
such a distinguished and influential recruit for their hard-pressed
cause. Rancé was in favour with the royal family, a personal friend
of Cardinal de Retz, and of numerous bishops and high government officials. Early in September 1664 he found himself on the
way to Rome, with another abbot, to plead the cause of the
reform before the Pope. He did not return to la Trappe until
April 1666. In fact the mission failed, but it must be counted as
the first real test of his vocation that he was involved in the world
of ecclesiastical power politics before he had had time to settle
down to monastic life. Unlike some of the reforming leaders, who
spent so much time intriguing in Paris that their abbeys fell into
neglect, Rancé rejected this temptation. It is quite likely, but not
certain, that he would still have rejected it had the mission to
Rome been successful.

The next temptation was similar, but more insidious. The battle
over autonomy for Reformed Cistercians had been lost in Rome,
but there was still something to fight for in France, especially by
playing off the King against the Pope. Moreover, as Rancé became
more personally and directly involved in the reform of la Trappe,
which very soon became flourishing and famous, it could be plau-
sibly represented to him that the future of the whole reform,
including his own abbey, was at stake. One after another the
temptations of campaigning were met and overcome. He spoke
once, and once only, at a General Chapter at Cîteaux on behalf
of the reform; he never attended another. He refused the important post of Visitor offered by the Abbot of Cîteaux. After reluctantly attending various assemblies of reform leaders, who would
have liked him to take over command, and after sending a powerful letter to the King in defence of their cause, finally, in 1675,
when all efforts had failed, he came back from Paris vowing never
again to leave the gates of his monastery – a vow which he kept
to the letter, except for three brief visits to a convent not far
away. One has only to read his letters, and contemporary
accounts, to see what pressures were put on him to accept high

office in the order, and how consistently he refused, always declaring that he regarded his abbey as his tomb and wanted only to live his life of penance there in humble obscurity. This was no false modesty, but an absolute conviction that his call had been to la Trappe and nowhere else.

Certain aspects of the life led there, and of his own in particular, cast light on the conversion which finally brought him to it. The most celebrated, perhaps most typical, feature of life at la Trappe was physical austerity. The reform sought to abolish all the mitigations introduced in the course of the centuries into the original Cistercian rule. In particular they practised, and attempted to impose on the whole order, perpetual abstinence from meat, fish and eggs (whence their nickname of Abstinents), a rigorous rule of silence and enclosure, and stricter rules on dress. Such a rule might be regarded as satisfying the most exigent demands of penance, but it did not satisfy Rancé. With the eager support of his brethren he intensified the austerity by taking the dietary rules to the limits of endurance, by imposing on all (including himself) the obligation of manual labour, by restricting access to the single room kept warm by a stove, by cutting down on sleep and rest. In a word, he made no concession of any kind to bodily frailty. At the same time he only authorized the use of extra penitential practices, like the scourge or wearing of hairshirts, in exceptional cases, and no retreats were held at la Trappe, on the grounds that the daily life allowed of no intensification. In letters to men and women in religion he constantly stressed the importance of strict obedience to their rule, whatever it might be, and the danger of personally chosen deviations from it towards additional austerity. He was a sound enough psychologist to know that singularity, even in austerity, encourages pride, where unquestioning conformism promotes both humility and solidarity.

Inevitably such a regime, and the much-publicized mortality rate, led to charges of what would now be called a death wish, and in a literal sense these cannot be refuted. Rancé and his monks welcomed death as the beginning of a new, eternal life, but it cannot be stressed too much that what they longed to escape from in life was not the hardship they so joyfully bore in common but the lurking occasion of sin. In their eyes sin was not the familiar wickedness of the outside world but, always and above all, self-indulgence, pride, *amour-propre*. Monotony and physical deprivation freed them from themselves for the total service of God, and what Rancé constantly referred to as 'the cause of Jesus Christ'.

This attitude was reinforced by another feature of life at la Trappe which was no less controversial for being less spectacular. From letters and other accounts it is clear that Rancé had always prohibited every form of intellectual activity, especially theology, and permitted only such devotional reading as the Desert Fathers and more modern works of piety. His own intelligence and learning were considerable, but by no means unique in the community, and the total sacrifice represented by this prohibition unquestionably proved harder than the physical austerities to him and others like him. It is a somewhat cruel irony that the dogmatic extension of this ban on studies to all true religious, when he published a chapter on it in his book on monastic life, *De la Sainteté et des Devoirs de la Vie monastique* (*On the Sanctity and Duties of the Monastic Life*) (1683), provoked a violent controversy which lasted more or less until his death and led him to a display of impressive erudition, as well as regrettable intolerance. Such defects of character – for they are that – give an insight into his conversion, and its limits. Pride, not materialism or carnality, was Rancé's chief sin; he was quite right to denounce himself as a sinner, but quite wrong in supposing that the righteousness of his cause (even if conceded) justified the tone he used towards his opponents and critics. That there was a demon of aggression inside him seems undeniable, but the record shows that once he was in the presence of his adversary his natural charm and charity broke through.

This unattractive side of his character must be seen in perspective. His conversion explicitly involved obscurity. He wanted to be left alone to practise penance according to his lights. Unfortunately his fame spread too widely to allow this. He always believed himself to be right, but in maintaining and illustrating that belief in practice he inevitably implied that others were wrong. He remained judicially subject to the authorities of his order, but secured grudging permission to observe the rule at la Trappe more strictly than it was observed anywhere else. He accepted, and encouraged, men to come from his own and other orders to seek a 'more perfect' life at la Trappe, and in so doing became involved in some very acrimonious disputes with superiors unwilling to recognize themselves as imperfect. Prevailed upon by friends, quite probably against his own original inclinations, he published his book on monastic life, setting up the regime at la Trappe as the basis for any 'true' monastic observance. To the numerous aggrieved victims of his criticism he seemed merely arrogant and opinionated, but in his own terms he was not defending his opinion or taste; he was justifying nothing less than his own conversion and its continuing effects on those who came to share it with him. The categorically imperative call he had heard after six long years' search could not be open to discussion. A call is obeyed, or rejected, not modified; the truth for the believer either is, or is not. Rancé, like Pascal, perhaps like all converts, could not compromise and survive, and when he claimed to be defending the cause of Christ, rather than his own judgment, he meant what he said. But that granted, he can still not be absolved from pride.

So what did he do about it? The first point to make is that he always spoke for his whole community, and recognized that the validity of the way of life practised at la Trappe depended on them, not just on him. One has only to read the numerous *Relations* he composed on the death of individual religious to see that his pride in their example is that of an officer privileged to command outstanding troops (the comparison was in fact made in the first published description of la Trappe, by Félibien).

The second, harder, point is that up to his death he never ceased harping on the statement made in his letter of 1664: no penance could adequately atone for his sins, and only death could release him from temptation. As the years went on it is clear that he is not speaking wholly, or mainly, of past sins, but rather of continuing pride, ingratitude, faltering love; twenty-five years spent entirely within the monastery walls left little enough scope for other kinds of sin. He refers often enough to the peace enjoyed by particular monks for his own lack of inner peace to be apparent. His driving, restless personality might well have accepted submersion in silent anonymity, but circumstances, superiors and misguided friends conspired to rob him of such peace, and even when he laid down the burden of the abbacy his remaining five years were sadly disturbed by domestic dissension around him.

Finally, to offset these two negative facts, the most positive result of the conversion in the long run – thirty-six years is long by any standards – is the extraordinary insight it gave him into the lives and problems of the innumerable men and women who came to him for help. Not only virtuous recruits presented themselves, but also men of truly scandalous life, who made reparation and found peace at la Trappe. His sympathy for such men, for women like Mère Louise and Louise de la Vallière, repenting as a Carmelite nun for her career as royal mistress (worldly, but not remotely discreditable by secular standards), for others still in the world wrestling with their consciences, in a word for his fellow sinners, such sympathy is without reserve, and buttressed by stout hope and encouragement. He was a staunch friend, in some cases for fifty years or more, and one of his most attractive, not to say Christian, qualities is his capacity for affection and concern, on occasion for people he did not even know personally. The gift for friendship is attested in the time before his conversion; the concern for all those in need certainly came after.

The frequency with which certain images and expressions recur in Rancé's letters is as good an indication of the *form* of his conversion as his actual conduct. From the very first he spoke of his days being numbered, his death imminent; he writes of the prodigious speed with which time passes, bringing us dizzily to judgment and eternity; he compares our life to a bird on the bough, to a fleeting breath. Not just the fact of death, but the ineluctable challenge of eternity and the totally precarious state of our earthly existence are what preoccupy him, perhaps even more than the thought of sin. The other favourite images are those of the storm followed by safe arrival in harbour. His own tempestuous nature needs no further emphasizing (and Bremond's cleverly malicious book *L'Abbé Tempête*[3] has given it wider currency), but the image is incomplete without the subsequent calm. All in all it seems hardly doubtful that Mme de Montbazon's sudden death shocked him into a realization that (as he says so often) the account may be demanded of us at any moment, and to be unprepared is to be too late. Whether it was fear about her fate, knowing her as he did, horror at his own narrow escape from a sudden death cutting short a futile life, or some combination of the two, coupled with an overwhelming sense of guilt, his feelings at this initial conversion of 1657 seem to have persisted.

Evidence of this seems to be reflected and clarified in the numerous references in letters written over the years to cases of sudden death, particularly affecting men and women of notably worldly habits and above all ecclesiastics of less than exemplary lives, like his own uncle, the Archbishop of Tours. He never fails to comment on the horror of being thus caught unprepared for the final reckoning. But this gloomy picture has a positive side. Those whom Rancé sees as, like himself, reprieved from the consequences of their sins, may hope for eternal peace after atoning on earth. To many others he writes that they have enjoyed God's grace from early childhood and should give thanks accordingly. All, however, regardless of their response, he considers called by Christ to his service, which means uncompromising renunciation of worldly values. Christ, though, is more than

Saviour, and a phrase (from a letter to the Carmelite niece of the great soldier Turenne) is especially revealing: 'Jesus Christ alone is worthy of our attachment. He is the only friend for all times and all ages.'[4] It is certainly remarkable how often Rancé brings in the name of Jesus in letters to all kinds of correspondent, and usually as master and shepherd rather than as victim on the cross.

It was the second conversion of 1662–3 which gave Rancé his rule of life, his sense of responsibility for and solidarity with others, the confidence that the voyage might be stormy but that the landfall would bring calm. The polemic, the touchiness, the obstinacy arise from the need he felt to defend his position, not from any personal considerations, and his own peaceful end vindicates the sound and fury that so often preceded it.

6

JOHN BUNYAN

To write of Bunyan's conversion is to write of Bunyan's whole life and work. The countless editions and translations of the *Pilgrim's Progress* (said to exist in a hundred languages) must make it a work of comparable importance to that of the *Imitation of Christ*, one of the first best-sellers of printing, but the shadowy figure of Thomas à Kempis is almost equal in biographical obscurity with that of the legendary tinker of Bedford. Giant Despair and Mr Valiant-for-Truth are far better known than Bunyan's two wives, four children or numerous persecutors, and yet the life is the man, the allegory with all its vivid images is firmly grounded in Bunyan's experience.

John Bunyan was born in 1628, in the same decade therefore as Pascal and Rancé, in the village of Elstow, just outside Bedford. His father seems to have come from a farming family fallen on hard times, and exercised the humble, but respectable, trade of brazier, repairing metal utensils in homes round about, but by no means the itinerant tinker of legend. Next to nothing is known of his childhood; he went to school, where he learned at least to read and write, and he was prone to vivid dreams and visions. He was probably mustered for the army when he was sixteen, in about 1644, and was discharged two or three years later. Very soon afterwards, about 1648, he married, but even his wife's name is unknown. He speaks of her father as a 'godly' person, but in terms suggesting that he never knew him. Poor as they were, his wife brought to their household two books which they would read together, *The Plain Man's Pathway to Heaven* and the *Practice of Piety*.

Their first child, Mary, was born blind in 1650, and was followed by Elizabeth, John and Thomas. Apparently under his wife's influence he began the outward practice of religion, going to church (Anglican, of course) twice a day, and holding offices and ceremonies in particular esteem, but in his account he assigns this period to his sad and sinful state.

About 1651 he met John Gifford, founder of the Bedford Separatist Church, and for the next two or three years underwent a period of intense spiritual crisis, wrestling with despair and temptation which he describes in detail in his autobiography. By 1655 he had come to some kind of equilibrium, for he was received into the Bedford congregation, with baptism by total immersion, and began to preach the following year. This was a so-called 'open communion' church, in which total immersion baptism was a token of membership, but not a condition of Christian fellowship.[1] 'Faith in Christ and holiness of life, without respect to this or that circumstance, or opinion, in outward and circumstantial things' were the only conditions, but members were 'required to have undergone a conversion of the classic Puritan type, following on a conviction of their own unworthiness . . . Evidence for the genuineness of the experience was provided by their testimony before the meeting. . . ' The existence and example of this practice are of manifest importance in assessing the form and stages of Bunyan's conversion.

He soon began to make a name for himself in Bedford, whither he moved from Elstow in 1655, by public disputes, especially with Quakers, whose reliance on an inner light he regarded as simply blasphemous. He also began to write pamphlets and longer works, amongst which may be mentioned the memorably entitled *A Few Sighs from Helle, or the Groans of a Damned Soul* (1658), and *The Doctrine of the Law and Grace Unfolded* (1659). In 1659 he married again (it is not known when his first wife died; his father had incidentally set a precedent by marrying three times), this time to a woman called Elizabeth.

In the normal course of events he would no doubt have pursued a local and perhaps national career as preacher and writer, bringing up his family in modest but serene circumstances, and would have lived and died like countless other virtuous non-conformists long since forgotten by history. Beyond Bedford, however, the tide of politics was running against him, and a spiritual evolution which had found no hindrance under the Commonwealth met an insuperable obstacle in the Restoration of 1660. Bunyan was arrested, convicted of holding a conventicle and sent to jail (the maximum penalty was transportation). There he stayed for some twelve years, and although the conditions of his captivity were sufficiently flexible to allow him to attend services in Bedford, and even to go to London on occasion, he was at best a prisoner on parole.[2] 'At any time, merely by undertaking not to preach again to a public assembly, Bunyan might have obtained his release: this is a measure of his courage and of the degree of personal integrity he had achieved once his religious doubts were at rest.'

During this long period of confinement he wrote his spiritual autobiography, *Grace Abounding to the Chief of Sinners*, and, as now seems virtually certain, *The Pilgrim's Progress*. In 1677 he spent another six months in jail, and as *Pilgrim's Progress* was published in 1678, it is still held by some scholars that its composition dates from this second incarceration. Now, however, that documentary evidence has been found proving that on this second occasion Bunyan spent no more than six months a prisoner, it seems much more likely that he wrote his masterpiece during the long years of his earlier sentence. It is part of the legend that the actual prison was the small lock-up which used to stand on the bridge at Bedford, but being convicted at the County Assizes Bunyan was certainly housed in the more commodious, if less picturesque, county gaol.

After his final release in 1678 he led much the sort of life he would have led but for his original imprisonment. His preaching and pastoral visits in and around Bedford established him as the leading Dissenter of the region; he was frequently engaged in dispute with divines of other persuasions, including academics from Cambridge, and seems to have held his own, even if he did not lack enemies, public and private. In 1688 he was taken ill while on a visit to London, where his congregation had close contacts with similar believers, and died peacefully at the home of a friend, a grocer on Snow Hill. In 1692 his wife followed him. An impressive portrait of him survives.

By birth and education he was destined to be the victim rather than the shaper of social and political circumstances, and by temperament he was hardly cut out for the role of a Penn or a Wesley, but the mark he made by his work – and still indirectly makes – is uniquely and indelibly his. Though his writing is in the general Puritan tradition, the fusion of experience and expression has enabled it to be read over the centuries as one man's witness, independent of any specific context. The limitations of Bunyan's early education and subsequent reading partly explain the overwhelming influence of the Bible and absence of literary affectation, but this he shared with his invariably humble co-religionaries. He gives a more cogent reason in his preface to *Grace Abounding*:[3]

> God did not play in convincing of me; the Devil did not play in tempting of me; neither did I play when I sunk as into a bottomless pit, when the pangs of hell caught hold of me: wherefore I may not play in my relating of them, but be plain and simple, and lay down the thing as it was.

It is instructive to compare the explicitly autobiographical account given in *Grace Abounding* with the much more general allegory of *Pilgrim's Progress*. As Roger Sharrock points out in his excellent edition, *Grace Abounding* follows a conventional pattern, but deviates from it by allotting fully two-thirds of the space to conversion. Moreover, in this account of his temptations and despair, 'Bunyan is most personal and least influenced by traditional precedents'. The intensity of the two-year conflict is fully conveyed by Bunyan's account, notably free of the clichés from which he does not escape elsewhere, and Sharrock very pertinently observes: 'The exactness of his recreation of the life of the soul, is the result of his living over again the original experience.'[4] It was not enough to know that he was saved, he must constantly recall his old self in order to hold on to his new.

In his childhood, Bunyan tells us, he was conspicuous for 'cursing, swearing, lying and blaspheming', and already by the age of nine or ten afflicted with dreams, visions and terrors of hell. He was fully aware of sin, and went on sinning. Then come the ritual occasions of preservation from physical danger: two escapes from drowning, one from an adder, and one from a bullet on active service.

His marriage, as mentioned, brought him to the outward practice of religion, in retrospect described as superstition, but kept him heedless of the spiritual danger he was running. The first nudge towards conversion came in the form of a sermon Bunyan heard against Sabbath breaking, to which he was particularly prone, and the first twinge of personal guilt assailed him. Not for long, however, for later the same day he was taking part in a game of cat when he heard a voice from heaven calling him to account. His reaction was to return to the comforting despair of his sin. Only a month later his swearing and cursing brought him such a sudden rebuke from a woman of otherwise no special merit that he at once abandoned the habit.

The next stage was Bible reading – the historical part, he tells us, rather than Paul's epistles – and then, for over a year, a 'conversion from prodigious profaneness to something like a moral life',[5] as yet ignorant of Christ, grace, faith and hope. An odd consequence of this conversion was that he gave up his previously favourite pastimes of bell-ringing and then, after a year, dancing.

None of this availed him spiritually, until one day in Bedford he chanced to overhear some poor women talking about their new birth in Christ and the inadequacy of their own righteousness to do them any good. This encounter tipped the balance, his hardness of heart melted, and he began to think no longer of his moral life but of eternity; in more technical language, not of the law but of justification.

The section that follows this revelation fully conveys the spiritual torment and confusion of this phase in Bunyan's conversion. He describes, for example, how he was tempted to think that the only way he could test whether he truly had faith was by working some miracle. Accordingly, as he rode along a country lane, he proposed making the puddles dry and the dry places wet, but at the last moment shrank from putting his faith to such a test. He speaks, too, of a kind of vision in which he saw these poor believers of Bedford cut off from him by a mountain, through which he could only pass by squeezing through a narrow gap. He was perplexed to know whether he was among the elect, or whether it was now too late; he read the Bible from beginning to end to see whether God's promises had ever failed the righteous; he waited impatiently and uncertainly for Christ's personal call.

So far he had tried to work things out all by himself, but the next stage led him to talk to the poor believers, who in turn introduced him to their pastor, Mr Gifford. The worst of his crises now began. He could not believe that Christ had love for him, so convinced was he that his sin had cut him off. The profusion of concrete images of violence is notable – the tempest, the child thrown down, rent and torn by the Devil, breaking the gates of brass, sin bubbling up from his heart and so on. Momentary respite was brought by hearing a sermon on the words (from the Song of Solomon) 'my love', but soon the torments returned, with visual and aural hallucinations. From atheism to blasphemy, from doubt to despair, Bunyan ran the whole gamut of temptation and dereliction. No sin so caught his guilty imagination as that against the Holy Ghost, the sin of final despair from which there is no deliverance. His eyes were even too dry for tears. In this pitiful state he endured about a year. Gradually he found peace and reconciliation, always, it seems, in meditating some particular text of scripture. The final stage of his recovery came from finding one day a battered copy of Luther's *Commentary on Galatians* (translated into English already in 1575), of which he says 'I do prefer this book . . . (excepting the Holy Bible) before all the books that ever I have seen as most fit for a wounded conscience.'[6]

The outstanding feature of Luther's book, omitting the virulent attacks on the Pope and Romish abuses, is his identification of the Law of Moses as spiritually destructive, and the absolute, exclusive insistence on faith in Christ's saving grace. In theological, intellectual terms the argument is not hard to follow, but translated into spiritual, psychological experience, and specifically that of two or three years of anguished conflict, it can only have such meaning as any given reader's experience supplies. Faith is as elusive a concept as love, and measured by the literal yardstick of Bunyan's biblical interpretation would seem almost impossibly elusive. Yet in a manner which he succeeds in communicating, through tone rather than fact, Bunyan knew when he at last held the faith he had sought for so long. By the same token he knew when it suddenly vanished, and once more this happened.

For two years he was obsessed with the image of Esau selling his birthright, of selling Christ (in his own words), despite short-lived relief derived from the promises of Christ's redeeming blood. From one morbid self-accusation to another Bunyan convinced himself that while even the most heinous offences against the Law were forgivable through Christ, he had been guilty of that sin of 'blaspheming against the Holy Ghost, [which] hath never forgiveness, but is in danger of eternal damnation' (Mark 3). His appalling crime was, he believed, to have succumbed to the temptation of saying of Christ 'let him go if he will'. If the cause was all in the mind (or spirit), the effects were dramatically psychosomatic: fits of trembling, weeping, nervous prostration, inability to eat or sleep, frequent hallucinations, feeling an outcast even among the people of God, fanciful tests and consultations, the full array of advanced pathological anxiety. The clinical precision of the description should make psychiatric diagnosis easy: 'My peace would be in and out sometimes twenty times a day: Comfort now and Trouble presently; Peace now, and before I could go a furlong, as full of Fear and Guilt as ever heart could hold;'[7] this state continued for seven weeks.

Eventually the storm subsided, and Bunyan speaks of a sweet and blessed comfort lasting a good twelve months. Interestingly he himself offers two reasons for this very long period of temptation: one that he prayed only for deliverance from present troubles, and not from future temptation; the other that he tempted God by attaching, as he put it, an 'if' to the all-seeingness of God. The example he gives of the latter is an occasion during his wife's pregnancy when she was in great pain and he secretly prayed that she might be cured so that he would then know that God knew his innermost thoughts. It seems odd that he should have doubted for a moment that God knows our hearts and minds, and odd too that he should not simply have prayed for his wife's relief instead of striking a kind of bargain with God, but this is what he records, and we must believe him.

He also goes on to assess the lessons and advantages he ultimately gained from all these trials. First, feeling cut off from Christ, he recognized the truth of that which caused him such terror, whereas his earlier doubts had inclined him to atheism, and second, it gave him a much keener appreciation of scripture and the nature of the promise: 'I saw that the truth and verity of them were the keys of the kingdom of Heaven; those that the Scriptures favour, they must inherit bliss; but those that they oppose and condemn must perish for evermore.'[8] Certainly both these lessons figure very prominently in *Pilgrim's Progress*, and the latter seems to provide an explicit answer to the danger of pure subjectivity inherent in the kind of spiritual crisis to which Bunyan and his fellow believers were so prone. His conclusion is: 'I never saw those heights and depths in grace, and love, and mercy as I saw after this temptation.'

Inevitably other trials beset him, probably until the moment of his death, but for him deliverance from the great temptation constituted the final stage in his conversion after which he was able to lead a properly Christian life and exercise his ministry. As one might expect, he regarded himself as profoundly unworthy, but moved both by the recognition that gifts are meant to be used and by the evident edification of his hearers, he came to accept that God wished to use him for his own inscrutable ends. At first he preached on guilt and hell, on which he felt he had special authority, but after about two years began to speak more positively of Christ's benefits to the world. Revealingly, he admits that he felt a special attraction for 'awakening', rather than preaching to the converted, and could not be satisfied 'unless some fruits did appear in my work'.[9] At the same time he was wise enough not to glory in his gifts, and tempted often enough in exercising them (even if he did not fall) to avoid complacency. Thus his resisting temptation led Satan to devise other means of nullifying his ministry, and in a remarkably comprehensive phrase he reports rumours that he was 'a Witch, a Jesuit, a Highwayman and the like'.[10] Particularly offensive were charges regarding his sexual conduct, which he most solemnly refutes. Even in jail his temptations were extreme, and he describes how, when it seemed quite likely he would end on the gallows, he was tormented by fears of such cowardice and would publicly disgrace his faith. Fortunately he was never put to that test.

In Bunyan's own account the period of his conversion seems to have begun with the first faint stirrings of guilt prompted by the sermon on Sabbath-breaking, presumably in about 1650, and to have reached some conclusion (though in one sense it never ended) in about 1655, when he was received into the Bedford congregation. The central period of two or three years, during which the violence of the conflict almost destroyed him, has no well-defined beginning and end, and seems to have included numerous momentary respites (as when he read Luther on Galatians) preceding fresh relapses. As a matter of common human experience one can see how an outwardly moral and religious life could be consistent with the most chaotic spiritual state, even though the opposite is not true. Swearing and Sabbath-breaking were occasions for public scandal and as such had to be given up for themselves; bell-ringing and dancing were inoffensive pastimes which he gave up rather as people give up sweets or tobacco in Lent. Once he had rejected the Law as irrelevant, even hostile, to salvation, Bunyan made it impossible for any outsider to judge his spiritual state except by the external manifestations of acute distress, groaning, insomnia and the like. But such manifestations represent conflict, not necessarily defeat by temptation, and in the last analysis he and he alone could declare the outcome. We know he talked to Gifford and other believers during his torments, and his wife must have been the anguished witness of many harrowing scenes. Yet he explicitly states at the point where his self-examination leaves a little room for hope that he had never publicly declared the despair concerning Christ's love for him which he took to be that ultimate and unforgivable sin against the Holy Ghost. By the time temptation had passed he could talk and write about it, but one can appreciate the paralysing isolation in which he must have found himself during the years of trial. Whatever one may think of the theology of Catholic and Anglican sacraments, they do undeniably relieve some of the psychological strain, and claim, of course, to be means of grace. This brings us back to the point already made: only when Bunyan's obsessive scrutiny of scripture convinced him that an authentic message of salvation addressed to him personally lay in specific texts, only then did he yield to hope. Conversion thus meant for him a recognition of congruity between the transcendental word of God and his inner spiritual dispositions. His steadfastness during the twelve years in prison is the fruit of this conversion.

All this shows a very different emphasis from that to be found in the *Pilgrim's Progress*, though the raw materials are recognizably similar. The full title of that famous book at once makes the point: *The Pilgrim's Progress from This World to That Which is to Come*. In other words the end, in glory, determines the shape and value of all that leads up to it. *Grace Abounding* contains sections on Bunyan's ministry and imprisonment, but the full title again reflects the emphasis: '*to the Chief of Sinners*', and while a blessed end is implied, the portion of the journey studied is chronologically very brief.

The most immediately obvious stylistic feature of *Pilgrim's Progress* is, as in any allegory, the exteriorization of qualities and psychological phenomena. Somehow the tethered lions and the bleached bones, the lethal quagmire and the sulphurous mouth of Hell, the foul fiend Apollyon and the Giant Despair, with his faintly absurd wife Diffidence, touch the imagination rather than the emotions, like mediaeval sermons in stone and glass. If we did not know the intolerable suffering behind these fairy-tale images we should react to them as to the witches and wolves of Grimm or Hans Andersen. More impressive is the sinister trial at Vanity Fair before Judge Hategood and the villainous panel of jurors, more terrifying indeed than the hideous death inflicted on Faithful, for the intensity of malevolence there depicted bears the unmistakable stamp of experience. A comparison with Bunyan's *Relation of his Imprisonment*, and his wife's attempt to move the judges, shows that memory, not invention, inspired the account.

Oddly perhaps, memory of known experience often produces a somewhat flat effect. The man in the Iron Cage, seen at the Interpreter's House, and identified as being guilty of the sin against the Holy Ghost, is no more than a museum piece, because Christian is a mere spectator of an agony which Bunyan himself had undergone. There is, in a word, no identification at the affective level between Christian and the author, and if there is such identification with the reader it is somehow different.

As far as general themes go, the Christian journey, and to that extent conversion, is represented by two features which barely figure in *Grace Abounding*. The first is alienation from the world and its ways, an idea constantly conveyed by meetings and discussions with stereotypes of unregenerate life like Wordly-Wise-man, Talkative and Ignorance, all of whom exert the strongest pressure on Christian to follow their example. The second is complementary, and is the very positive theme of solidarity illustrated at every step of the journey by such companions as Hopeful and Faithful (and, in the second part, Mr Valiant-for-Truth). In the autobiography other figures do appear, like Gifford and the poor believers, but the claustrophobic impression of isolation and alienation in a technical sense predominates in the central part. The inner awareness of sin and its ravages could never have such general application as the animated cartoon of human types performing against a topography of spiritual allegory, but the real difference derives from treating the uniquely personal experience of conversion in one book and the whole of the Christian life in the other.

The actual start of Christian's journey corresponds to the initial stages of Bunyan's conversion in somewhat stylized form. He begins by asking 'What shall I do to be saved?' and at last meets Evangelist, who tells him to flee from the wrath to come. After vainly trying to persuade wife and family to accompany him (Part II is devoted to their less hair-raising journey in his footsteps), Christian rushes off as one demented shouting: 'Life, life, eternal life!' Passing the Slough of Despond, one of his first trials is escaping from the mountain that threatened to crush him, which Evangelist, quoting Galatians, interprets as Mount Sinai and the Law. Going in through the Strait Gate (recalling Bunyan's vision of the poor believers of Bedford whom he could join only by squeezing through a narrow gap), Christian spends a while at the Interpreter's House, learning the truth of scripture, and it is only on leaving there that he arrives at the Cross by the wayside. There his crushing burden of guilt slips off, he is given new clothes and a roll with a seal, his passport. Thus far his trials have been relatively few, and some three-quarters of the book is yet to come, but this is strictly all we are told about his conversion. Only in the last quarter of the book does Christian, now accompanied by Hopeful, fall into the hands of Giant Despair at Doubting Castle, and if this is their sorest trial it is also almost their last. Consequently despair in *Pilgrim's Progress* is more a test of perseverance after conversion, and all the fatigues of the Christian life, than a primary condition of conversion itself. One can see how twelve years in prison would teach the value of perseverance, but one can see too that victory in the earlier spiritual conflict furnished the strength to persevere.

Faith came hard to Bunyan, but when he overcame his temptations of doubt and despair he found justification in the saving blood of Christ, and this is largely what the record of his conversion in *Grace Abounding* tells us. Once justified, he went on to sanctification in his witness, as preacher and prisoner, and the Christian (and his wife Christiana) of the *Pilgrim's Progress* is the typical, humble man or woman of his flock to whom he announced the glory to come. By taking the two books together we get a truer picture than by separating one from the other.[11] 'To the Puritan the regeneration of the individual soul was the central fact of religious experience'; each of us must seek his own salvation, but in the common and unique saviour will be found a pattern intelligible to all. It is not from standard literary models like Augustine, but from daily wrestling with the literal text of scripture and daily examination of his conscience that Bunyan composed both the experience and the account of his conversion. His voices, good and evil alike, spoke the language of scripture; his vivid imagination and probably morbid sensibility did the rest.

7

WILLIAM BOOTH

Few religious bodies of today are so intimately associated with conversion as their end and their means as the Salvation Army. Other missionary bodies are naturally concerned to convert unbelievers, and to follow up conversion by ministering to them, but the Salvation Army has such a very special understanding of what conversion entails, which converts to seek, and how to deal with them that it stands apart from other bodies doing similar work. Changes in society have inevitably affected the Salvation Army, but its spirit derives from the personality and life of its founder to such an extent that without him it could no more be explained than Franciscans without Francis or Jesuits without Ignatius. Fortunately, so much is known about William Booth, founder and first General, that there is little room for argument as to his intentions over a long, well-documented life.

William Booth was born in Nottingham on 10 April 1829, the third of five children of Samuel Booth and Mary Moss, his much younger second wife. Samuel had formerly been very prosperous, and though reduced in circumstances sent his son to the best available local school. William's recollections of his father were hazy, and generally unfavourable, giving the impression that Samuel had no real contact with his family and cared only about money. As for Mary, apparently of partly Jewish origin, she seems to have been eclipsed by her husband and perpetually worried about his finances. The boy grew up, so far as one can judge, without much or any parental affection and, on his own later admission, with no effective religious training, though he attended church and Sunday school as was usual in those days.

When William was thirteen the long-feared financial collapse at last took place. His father was finally ruined, took William away from school and apprenticed him to a pawnbroker. For a boy of that age to be confronted in his daily life with such a harrowing proof of money's power, and the wretchedness of poverty, can only have been a formative experience of great significance. Although it seems that at the time he took his trade in quite a matter-of-fact way, he later came to view it with revulsion. As if this were not enough, within a year, in September 1842, his father fell ill and, after belatedly making his peace with God, died, surrounded by his family singing 'Rock of Ages'.

From this time on William began to think about religion, and, under the influence of friends, to frequent the Wesleyan chapel rather than the parish church he had previously attended. His hours of work allowed him scant leisure, and his later memories supply few details for the context of what happened next. At eleven o'clock one night in 1844 he had what he regarded as a conversion experience out in the street, by the chapel, telling him to renounce sin and specifically to give back a silver pencil-case he had acquired from friends by questionable means. Once he had made this restitution, he recalled much later, he felt an immediate lightening of conscience and a new freedom to serve God.

It is obviously impossible to reconstruct the feelings of a fifteen-year-old boy from such slight evidence, particularly as William Booth passed on these recollections only when the subsequent course of his career encouraged him to read history backwards and thus see this incident as the first link in a chain of momentous importance. Two things, however, seem certain: his sense of sin and release, and his increasingly active participation in religion. It must also be relevant that at this time he enjoyed the close friendship of Will Sansom, a boy of his own age, more affluent but equally devout, and underwent his first mild emotional attachment to a girl. The affective development which his family had failed to promote in childhood was now in adolescence finding alternative means of expression.

Revivalism in various forms, legacy of the Wesleys and the earlier Quakers, was still very much a feature of the religious life of the age. In 1846 William Booth had attended the mission of a well-known visiting American evangelist when he fell ill, possibly due to over-excitement. Will Sansom, his friend, began an open-air mission in the poor quarters of Nottingham and invited William to join him as soon as health permitted. Whatever obscurity may veil the reality of the pencil-case incident, the events of 1846 are perfectly clear, and mark the beginning of his vocation. William's health improved, he joined his friend's group, and after some hesitation began to preach in the streets and at house meetings. All agree that he was at that time very earnest, and humourless, but an impressive speaker. His message was simple and basic: abandon sin and be saved by faith in Christ from otherwise inescapable hell.

He was then, and for a long time to come, a typical Wesleyan, with the doctrines and priorities of that movement, distinguished only by his preference for addressing the less prepossessing members of society. Early in his preaching career he made local history by bringing into the chapel, packed for Sunday service by the respectable pillars of Methodist society, a band of ragged youths from the slums, whom he placed in seats cheek by jowl with solid citizens. He was firmly instructed after this incident that he was not to repeat such conduct, but if such socially undesirable persons were to share in the worship they should in future be seated out of contact, indeed out of sight, of those whose cleanliness proclaimed their godliness. It is easier to be democratic in a society where soap and running water are available to all, and if Booth's outcasts cannot have been any dirtier than those of apostolic or mediaeval times, it is fair to stress the physical, as well as the social, implications of his initiative. It seems that he took the point as far as the chapel was concerned.

The Wesleyan authorities did not encourage, or even approve, Booth's youthful campaign in the streets, and his remaining family (his mother and two sisters at home), partly dependent on his small wages, were even less enthusiastic. It must have taken great courage, and vast expenditure of nervous energy, for an adolescent working a long hard day at the pawnshop to devote himself in the evening and on Sundays to saving others less fortunate than himself. He never doubted later that his capacity to perform this task was the outcome of an authentic conversion, which he tried to pass on to others. A biographer who knew him personally, H. L. Begbie, writes:

> 'Conversion with him was the divine focus revealing all thoughts and all things in their absolute perspective . . . He held . . . that directly a soul is converted – that is to say, directly the spirit of a man looks upon earthly life with the sure and certain knowledge that a living God exists, and that by faith in Christ he is brought into harmony with that God –

temptation loses its power and the soul is impelled towards
holiness.'[1]

This, a version of the Methodist doctrine of Entire Sanctification,
remained his belief throughout his life.

As can be seen, in such a view conversion is the new birth and
new life of the Christian, but it cannot be too strongly emphasized,
that the only alternative in Booth's very basic theology was quite
simply hell, everlasting damnation understood in the sense of real
torment rather than deprivation of bliss. This, the reality of hell,
is the essential counterweight to Booth's preaching of conversion,
but what gave his religion a special flavour from the start was the
literal and courageous interpretation he gave to Christ's redemptive work. Not only was no one, however depraved, to be denied
the chance of choosing salvation; those whom society despises
were from first to last his special targets. In his early years there
was an almost desperate nobility in such an attitude, which quite
clearly stems from the nature and circumstances of his own
conversion.

The original missionary spirit of the Wesleyans was far from
spent even fifty years after the founder's death (1791), and beside
the more sedate forms of worship, their services at this time
included invitation to sinners to confess their sins, to choose salvation and to come forward to the communion rail to declare
themselves before all. Thus conversion always remained a central
fact of Wesleyan worship and a major responsibility of ministers.
At nineteen William Booth was invited by the Superintendent of
the Circuit (regional senior minister) to consider entering the
ministry, but he refused, preferring to carry on as a lay preacher.
His apprenticeship to the pawnbroker over, he failed to find
reasonable employment in Nottingham and so in 1849 moved to
London in seach of work.

To his disgust the only work he could find was once more with
a pawnbroker, in Walworth, but very long hours and an uncon-
genial master did not prevent him from continuing to preach – a
letter of 1849 refers as to something quite usual to a sermon he
had recently preached of an hour and a half. The situation at this
time was complicated by dissensions resulting in schism within the
Methodist body. For various reasons Booth, originally on the side
of the traditionalists, was persuaded in 1851 to join the breakaway
Reformers as a full-time preacher, and then favourably to consider
entering the ministry. As if this decision were not momentous
enough, the very day he ceased his job with the pawnbrokers (10

April 1852, his birthday), he met and at once fell in love with his future wife, Catherine Mumford.

This young woman belonged to a type all too familiar in literature of the period. Rigorously puritanical as much by temperament as by upbringing, she was educated and intelligent, but subject to that indeterminate form of poor health from which, for example, Browning rescued his wife. An ardent feminist, apparently on good terms with her parents, she turned out to be exactly what Booth needed to develop within himself personal qualities which had been stunted by sheer material hardship coupled with affective impoverishment. In a practical way he was forced, first by the prospect and then the reality of domestic responsibilities, to weigh up any course of action with extreme care, and so obliged to define principles more clearly than ever before; psychologically, he had someone to consult whose judgment he respected, and whose future was involved in every decision. Catherine, too, undoubtedly gained from the association, not least because her own passionately held religious convictions could never have found such fulfilment as they did but for William.

The immediate consequences of his entry into full-time preaching were not very satisfactory, and after three months he was not invited to continue in London. He briefly toyed with the idea of joining the Congregational ministry, where each chapel was autonomous and not controlled by a central conference, as was the case with all the Methodist bodies. As soon as he got to know more about the Calvinist doctrine which he would, as a Congregationlist have had to profess and preach, he indignantly rejected it, choosing poverty with principles intact rather than a reasonably comfortable future without them. The sticking point, as he himself records, was the doctrine of election, the belief that only a select few can be saved and all the rest are damned no matter what they, or anyone else on their behalf, might do. Suddenly, when no employment seemed possible, he received an invitation to the important Spalding circuit in Lincolnshire, where he at once began to make his mark.

The very remarkable correspondence which ensued between William and Catherine, to whom he was now engaged, during the eighteen months of his Lincolnshire tour (up to January 1854), shows great development in his emotional life and more mature realization of his religious calling. He was still committed to revivalist methods, the vibrant appeal to sinners, but he now discussed the matter fully with Catherine, who raised questions and objections he had to answer. A striking phrase in an early letter (11 November 1852) illustrates his theology at the time: 'The great plan of salvation is, ceasing from making efforts to make unto yourself a righteous character and sinking helpless into the arms of Christ and accepting Full Salvation, a pure heart, and all the blessings of the New Covenant by faith.'[2] He goes on to admit his error in relying earlier on his own efforts. His own belief in Satan and hell, confirmed by his own experience of temptation, was only equalled in intensity by his gratitude for the atonement of Christ.

Early in 1854 he decided, after much hesitation, to become a theological student rather than continue with his now highly successful Lincolnshire mission. In February he returned to London, persevered with studies which irked his impatient soul, and on completion of his course was given permission to marry once he had served twelve months (instead of the usual four years) as assistant to an older minister in charge of a London circuit of the Methodist New Connection. His probationary year duly completed, he was married in June 1855. After a week's honeymoon the young couple went off to Guernsey for a revivalist campaign, and then William began travelling up and down the country, often without his wife, always short of money to support her and their regularly increasing family. His fellow ministers were divided as to the desirability of allowing him to continue his spectacular but unorthodox travelling campaign of revivalist preaching, and in 1857 appointed him to a circuit, that is a stable post, at Brighouse in Yorkshire. Next year, 1858, he received ordination as a fully-fledged minister, and was sent to Gateshead, where his wife created something of a sensation by speaking in public, with great success. However, William, with his wife's full support, grew ever more impatient with the restrictions put upon his evangelistic activities by the authorities of the New Connection, and at last, in July 1861, he resigned his ministry. Poor as his pay has been, it had kept him and his family (now four children) alive and reasonably secure, and the price of his independence was immediate and total insecurity.

Campaigns in Cornwall, and then in Cardiff, yielded the usual impressive statistics of conversions, while the Booths lived a hand-to-mouth existence, reliant on the unpredictable generosity of individual well-wishers. At the same time, hostility to William's methods hardened among all branches of the Methodist Church, and almost all chapels were closed to him. The deadlock was inevitable between his burning, even fanatical, sense of urgency in bringing sinners to Christ by highly emotional methods, and the long-term pastoral work of the resident circuit ministers who somehow had to follow up the initial impetus among such converts as well as seeing to the daily needs of their normally staid and respectable flock. Booth's sense of vocation was not compatible with any compromise of principle, but as yet no religious body could accommodate him.

Not long after the birth of their sixth child, in 1864, Catherine was invited to conduct a mission in Rotherhithe, in London, and what she saw there of the work being done among 'fallen women' persuaded her that they should move to London. Accordingly in 1865 the Booths took a house in Hammersmith, later moving to Hackney. In July 1865 William began a series of services in Whitechapel, in the East End, which marked the final stages on the road to what became the Salvation Army. At first he had envisaged the same kind of evangelism in which he had hitherto been engaged, addressing himself to the spiritual needs of the virtually pagan population of the slums, and sending converts on to church and chapel as appropriate.

Quite suddenly, it seems, he saw the situation in a different light. His wife records how he came home very late one night, quite overwhelmed by the pervading moral squalor of the streets in the East End through which he had passed, appalled by the universal hold that sin had over the wretched poor in the huge London slums, where alcoholism often began in early childhood and thieving took the place of education. He felt a quite specific call to devote himself to saving these lost multitudes, not by short-term skirmishes with evil, but by a full-scale war, which, as it turned out, was to last for the rest of his life.

Beginning in a tent in the Mile End Road, then using whatever premises he could hire, dance-halls, warehouses, anything, William Booth embarked on this new venture with undiminished enthusiasm, but against the most violent hostility, especially from the publicans, and indifference, often amounting to hostility, from church and chapel. Physical assault and real danger were the constant accompaniment to the back-breaking mission of Booth and his few supporters. The Christian Mission, as, after several changes of name, the organization was called, made a virtue out of necessity. Since existing religious bodies had reacted so unfavourably, Booth at last felt free to set up his own system.

From an early date he used converts to speak to meetings, and soon realized that this was immensely valuable both to the converts, who gained immeasurably in self-respect, and to the hearers, for whom the verifiable testimony of those who had so

recently been like them proved the reality of salvation. Drunk-
ards, bruisers, prostitutes, the roughest and most degraded members of society followed his call, and one picturesque
advertisement told of 'the milkman who never watered his milk
after he was saved'. The phrase 'saved to save' was always a
favourite of Booth's and sums up the imperative need for continuing action which he saw as the best remedy against complacency
and backsliding. He perceived that the one way in which he could
lastingly change men and women was to make them, from the
moment of their conversion, seekers and savers of the lost. The
Christian fellowship thus intimately associated with conversion
was reinforced by a common way of life: alcohol was renounced
(whence the fury of the drink trade), as were tobacco and all
kinds of frivolous entertainment; Sunday was strictly observed as
the Sabbath, and full participation in prayer and other meetings
was required. There was no room for passengers; all had to bend
their backs to the oars if the boat was not to founder.

From 1869, when Booth and his family began to distribute
Christmas dinners to the poor and then opened primitive eating-
houses called 'Food-for-the-Million Shops', the material needs of
the poor were recognized as an important element in the mission.
Meanwhile, in the ten years or so during which it assumed its
definitive form, Booth kept personal control of all that went on.
His long frustration as a Methodist had left him with complete
contempt for conferences and committees – he was wont to say
that if it had been left to a committee the children of Israel would
never have got across the Red Sea – and as General Superintendent his authority was supreme. Military metaphors had long been
part of his stock-in-trade, and the man-handling he and his followers so often had to suffer confirmed them in their view that
they were truly fighting a war against Satan, eternal life against
eternal damnation. It took some time to resolve on the strategy
of global warfare rather than that of sectarian consolidation of
local groups, but it was Booth who spurred the movement on. In
an address delivered to the conference of 1877 he described it as
a 'Council of War', but pronounced once and for all against ever
using conferences to legislate. His concluding words are revealing:
'Confidence in God and in me are absolutely indispensable both
now and ever afterwards.'[3]

The last step was taken in September 1878 when William Booth
was referred to as 'General of a Salvation Army' in the movement's magazine, and though his first reaction to the title was
disapproving (he found it pretentious and preferred 'Rev.'), from

then on the familiar military titles of the members and the movement came into force. By now the Army had 'stations' in most
large centres in England and South Wales, but had by no means
disarmed hostility, which in one famous case at Worthing actually
led to the reading of the Riot Act before an armed mob could be
dispersed. Interestingly in an article of January 1879 Booth quite
explicitly disclaimed any doctrinal innovation: 'We believe in the
old-fashioned salvation . . . Ours is just the same salvation taught
in the Bible . . . preached by Luther and Wesley and Whitefield
. . . purchased by the sufferings and agony and Blood of the Son
of God.'[4]

The introduction of the first uniforms, in 1880, and of brass
bands, about the same time (a factory was eventually set up to
produce instruments), the adaptation of popular songs to religious
words, the Salvation Army style as it is known today, followed
naturally from these beginnings. The formula brought rapid
growth – from fewer than a hundred in 1878 to about 16,000
officers when Booth died in 1912 – but it is also inevitably established the Army as a separate religious body, however harmonious
relations may have been at the individual or local level with
representatives of other churches. Together with the discipline,
authentically puritanical in its rigour and binding on all Salvationists and their families (officers have always been forbidden to
marry outside the Army), went an extreme form of revivalism, at
times approaching anarchy. The so-called 'Holiness Meetings', in
which Catherine and Bramwell, the eldest son, rather than William himself, took a leading role, provoked intense excitement
amounting to hysteria, with glossolalia and other Pentecostal
manifestations, encouraging excessive enthusiasm, but bringing
huge numbers of converts to the 'penitent-form' (Salvationist
equivalent of the Methodist communion-rail) to confess their sins
with sobs. That people needed a rude awakening is not in dispute,
that this was the right, let alone wisest, means of dispelling torpor
may be doubted. Many certainly found liberation from their over-
powering sense of guilt and sin, successors in this to the mental
and moral paralytics of the gospel miracles, many followed this
dramatic new birth with a new life, but from outside the proceed-
ings must have appeared to many, both Christian and sceptic, as
frightening and dangerous. It is only fair to balance this tendency
with the practical orders continually promulgated by the General
himself, a man full of common sense as well as ardour. He told
his followers as early as 1876 that their calling demanded above
all love: 'This love – this passion for souls – is the main-spring of

religious activity and the principle which governs all real and lasting work for God.'[5]

In 1881 General Booth took a decision which quite deliberately set the Army apart in both theory and practice from the other churches. Up to 1867 he had occasionally administered the sacrament of communion (in that year to his dying mother-in-law), and even later Salvationists quite often attended services of communion in church or chapel. In 1881, however, Booth, prompted by his son Bramwell and other younger men, decreed that henceforth sacraments, notably baptism and communion, would not be administered within the Army, which was correct from an ecclesiological standpoint as its members underwent no form of ordination, but neither should members, individually or collectively, receive those sacraments anywhere else. This was not just a matter of discipline, still less of personal taste, but a decision supported by Booth's assertion that scripture gave no authority for the belief that these, or any other, ceremonies were necessary for salvation, but, like the scripturally attested practice of ritual washing of feet, were just customs to be adopted or not at will. He was of course assuming a heavy responsibility, for instance with converts of Catholic origin, and apparently had occasional misgivings in later life, but it is noteworthy that he did not, as the Methodists had done, set up a schismatic sacramental or ministerial tradition. None the less, his decision once made had the same binding force on the Army as a papal decree on Catholics. For a former minister to take such a step, and in blank rejection of a démarche made by the Church of England at the highest level (the Archbishop of Canterbury through the Bishop of Truro), he must have had a quite exceptional degree of conviction of the rightness of his cause. He naturally became more autocratic with age and success, and enshrined in the Army's trust deed, as indeed he had done in that of the Christian Mission previously, not only his unchallenged authority as leader but his right, and that of all subsequent Generals, to nominate his successor. It was only at the end of Bramwell Booth's life that the present system of election was forcibly instituted against the General's protests at such disregard for his father's will.

This is not the place to recount the world-wide expansion of the Army, from America and Canada in 1880, to India in 1882, and thence to every part of the British Empire, to Japan and most parts of Europe. In extreme old age General Booth tried, and failed, to secure permission for a Russian branch, and on his deathbed he made his son, and successor designate, promise to carry the war to China. The activities always concentrated on the most despised members of society, prostitutes, vagrants, convicts (a particularly bold venture was in Cayenne, the French penal settlement), and came more and more to accompany spiritual and moral regeneration with practical provision of food, shelter and work. In one memorable article Booth compared the lot of the London poor with that of a cabhorse, guaranteed food and shelter so long as it was able to work, and demanded that the poor too should enjoy what he called 'the cabhorse charter'. Hostels, prisoners' aid societies, farming and industrial work, assisted emigration to the colonies were among examples of Booth's ceaseless campaign of salvation, which never stopped at handing out material relief but demanded material effort as the proof of spiritual cleansing. A book he published in 1890, written in collaboration with a journalist, offered a comprehensive solution to current social evils under the title *In Darkest England and the Way Out*. A conservative throughout his life, Booth loathed everything he knew of socialism and believed in a rather archaic paternalism. By a sad coincidence his wife died after long illness (cancer) just as he was completing the book. Her role as 'Mother of the Army' was in no way subordinate, and she commanded respect even from cultured persons, who often admired her more than her husband.

The list of world leaders Booth met and conquered in his later years is almost incredible. Edward VII and his Queen, the royal houses of Scandinavia, Cecil Rhodes and Winston Churchill, perhaps more remarkably Cardinal Manning and successive Archbishops of Canterbury, are among the most famous of those who were glad to pay him homage. When he died, blind and pathetically inactive, in 1912 he was given an official funeral procession through the City of London, of which he had been made a freeman, and tributes came from all over the world.

A century after its foundation the phenomenal success of the Salvation Army, which by one estimate may number as many as two million adherents of all ranks throughout the world (officers are of course much less numerous), bears continuing witness to the vision and faith of its first General. As is so often the case, however, the sheer scale and development of the movement can distract attention away from the spirit without which it would never have begun or survived. Obviously organizational ability and an exceptional personality were needed to transform a vision into a reality, faith into practical charity. Booth confounded his early critics, who prophesied that the public would soon tire of his methods, but those who vied with each other to pay him honour – the honorary DCL received at Oxford from the hands of the Chancellor, Lord Curzon, is the most agreeably incongruous – were recognizing the man and his achievement, the effective work being done under his direction amongst those whom governments and churches had shamefully neglected. They knew little or nothing of his modest beginnings and were principally glad to see someone else scavenging successfully the lower depths of society. If Salvationists do in fact save people socially, today this is still secondary to their spiritual mission, and it is the basis of that mission that deserves to be recognized and remembered.

Certain elements in William Booth's spiritual development call for comment. His initial conversion experience, the silver pencil-case incident, came at a very early age, fifteen, and seems to have preceded any perceptible affective development. The next stage of conversion, his beginnings as a preacher in 1846, is directly linked with his first recorded personal relationship outside the family, with Will Sansom, and at a time when his family relations were at best cordial and, in terms of understanding, minimal. He was lonely and in need of affection. It is noteworthy that his own poverty during so much of his life, well into middle age, did not warp him in any way, and on the contrary helped him to offer those less fortunate than himself what they, and he, needed most: not alms, but love.

Booth was a deeply emotional man, for whom the sight of suffering was almost intolerable, but it is clear that from his earliest days his conversion impelled him to give love rather than seek it. Like St Francis and Charles de Foucauld he saw his evangelistic vocation as being directed to the absolute outcasts of society, the moral lepers of his day, and his own unmistakable love and respect for them made credible his message of Christ's redeeming love. Even when he was forced into prominence he never lost the common touch, and accepted the honour paid to him as a means of furthering the work, not his own status. Right to the end of his life he waged war on sin, on the evil from which, he believed, each individual could choose deliverance if he wished. He did not try, or even want, to change society; he succeeded in changing those whose self-respect had been sapped by society's neglect and their own shame. His primitive theology was what these people needed, but the long years as a Methodist revivalist did not show him how to cure them permanently.

His marriage and responsibility for a family gave him a much more balanced emotional life, and also helped him to translate the message of conversion into an integrated way of life. His wife, and then his children, were part of his campaign, and his family's life of self-denial and service to others was not a refuge from endless war on sin but part of an essential GHQ. By sharing the hardships and social disabilities of those to whom he ministered, he closed the gap which so many other missionaries had perpetuated unwittingly by their methods. The strongly supportive nucleus he built up, first in the Christian Mission, then in the Salvation Army as finally constituted, was united by faith and love, but expanded and continued by common commitment to a life of quite specific work, under obedience, to which there could never be an end. Every sinner reconciled became a potential Salvationist, and, as with such modern movements as Alcoholics Anonymous, backsliding was checked because the ways of temptation were known to all and each gave the others strength. At the same time the doctrine of regeneration, 'washed in the Blood of the Lamb', meant that the converted sinners were proud to advertise the sin they had renounced, secure in their new Christian faith and fellowship with other cleansed lepers.

There is much to criticize on Booth's methods and teaching. For example, the dogmatic rejection of sacraments can be explained by the circumstances of the time, but may have impoverished the spiritual growth of the movement. Still, his obstinate battle against sin on the one hand and censoriousness on the other commands respect. When, after his wife's death, his relations with some of his children, and with some of the Salvationists overseas, reached breaking-point he never gave way to bitterness. He found love by giving it, and in some mysterious way his faith in Christ was never obscured by the vast organization he built up to meet the material needs of the poor. What sin he sought originally to expiate one cannot know, and if in later life he accused his adolescent self of worldliness, this may be verbal formality. It seems likely that a thirst for love, a realization of his emotional aridity, rather than any specific misdeed, brought him to Christ in the first place, and then to sinners equally deprived of love. Conversion was his whole life's work, and he made it a lasting reality for thousands.

8

CHARLES DE FOUCAULD

The life and character of Charles de Foucauld encompass such extremes and such paradoxes as to set him apart even from the other exceptional men and women discussed in these pages. Yet it is in this very respect that he exemplifies the phenomenon of conversion most clearly.

He was born in Strasbourg, of aristocratic family, in 1858 and had one sister, Marie, born in 1861. In 1864 he lost his mother and, only five months later, his father. One need subscribe to no particular psychological school to recognize the shattering impact of this double loss on so young a child. The two children were then brought up by their maternal grandfather, Colonel de Morlet, a kind and upright man, and also spent a good deal of time with their father's sister, Mme de Moitessier. It was the latter's daughter Marie (later to become Mme de Bondy) who, nine years older than Charles, was to become a second mother to him, and a decisive influence throughout his life.

The war of 1870 once more shattered stability, and the family had to move from Alsace to Nancy. There, in 1872, Charles made his first communion, but soon after began to doubt, 'despairing of the truth and no longer even believing in God, since no proof seemed sufficiently evident', as he wrote later. The aftermath of French defeat, his own adolescence, the loss in 1878 of his grandfather (and perhaps the marriage in 1874 of his cousin Marie), all contributed to a steady decline of moral effort. An undistinguished career as a cadet at St-Cyr, then as a cavalry cadet at Saumur, followed by a regimental posting in Lorraine, saw him deeply embedded in a life of indolent debauchery which brought him only melancholy and boredom instead of the distraction he craved.

In 1879 he took up with a young woman called Mimi, who accompanied him as unofficial wife when his regiment (now designated Chasseurs d'Afrique) went out in 1880 to Sétif in Algeria. Ordered to put an end to the public scandal, he refused and was suspended from duty. He retired with Mimi to Evian in March 1881, determined to live his own life in defiance of all social convention.

Suddenly events caught up with him. Less than three months after his suspension he read one day in the newspaper that his regiment was now engaged in operations in Algeria. He was allowed to rejoin them at once, and earned universal respect for his conduct on active service, both from his men and his brother officers. This was the end of the Mimi phase, and the first real contact with other men after all the years of empty socializing. After the campaign, which lasted only a few weeks, he began seriously to learn Arabic and Berber, and was at last rehabilitated in the eyes of his family.

While such a break with dissipation and moral inertia clearly marks a stage in Foucauld's development, it was essentially self-discovery rather than discovery of any external truth. His successive steps towards self-discovery uncannily foreshadow a future still distant, but it is only with hindsight that one can see the pattern forming. In 1882 he resigned from the Army, resolved to conduct his own exploration in Morocco, for which he felt powerful attraction. By now a serious Arabist, he set off disguised as an exiled Russian rabbi, in the company of a genuine North African rabbi, for a journey through Morocco lasting nearly a year, from June 1883 to May 1884. Often in danger of his life, subject to great mental and physical strain, he returned with a mass of highly professional observations and a profound respect for both Judaism and Islam. His interest in Morocco was, if anything, increased. It took him about a year to write up his report (subsequently published in 1886 as *Reconnaissance au Maroc*) and in 1885 it was hailed by the Geographical Society in Paris as a most distinguished piece of work. He had at last acquired the self-respect and recognition for lack of which his personality had for so long been in disintegration.

The long preliminary to full self-discovery began to end in 1886, when Foucauld took a flat in Paris, near Marie de Bondy and the church of St-Augustin. His flat, his dress (indoors at least) and his manner of life (he slept on the floor) were Arab, and he steeped himself in Arab culture and language. In addition, under his cousin's influence, he began to embrace chastity. One day in

October 1886 (most oddly he never recalled the actual date, between 27 and 30 of the month) he went into St-Augustin for a talk with the abbé Huvelin, whom he knew through his cousin and who enjoyed a wide reputation for being a remarkable spiritual director. Although, in his own account of the episode, he seems to have wanted no more than a chat, he finished on his knees making his confession, followed at once by communion on Huvelin's insistence. The conversion was total and unconditional. An interesting feature of his account, written in 1897, is that he lists at this point the many occasions of death from which God had thus far preserved him, lest he die in mortal sin, and they include accidents of riding and war, traditional elements of such accounts throughout the centuries.

His immediate and characteristically extreme reaction was to want to become a monk, but Huvelin was wise enough to make him wait while he attained clearer sight of his eventual vocation. Interestingly, there is a record in 1887 of Foucauld sending for Montalembert's *Les Moines dans l'Occident* and Arnauld d'Andilly's translation of *Lives of the Desert Fathers*, one of the first books Rancé read after his conversion (at just the same age). Three years went by, during which he made a pilgrimage to the Holy Land and visited various monasteries, including Solesmes and la Trappe, before he finally decided on the Trappist monastery of Notre-Dame-des-Neiges, in the Ardèche. This, the highest monastery in France, had a small dependent priory at Akbès in Syria, and here Charles de Foucauld believed himself called.

On 15 January 1890 he entered Notre-Dame-des-Neiges and was given the name of brother Marie-Albéric (modern Cistercians customarily prefix their individual names in religion with that of Mary); in June he set sail for Syria. J–F Six observes that 'one thing that made him suffer was having to obey',[1] and without Huvelin's firm guidance this passionate desire for independence could have been disastrous. Some three years after becoming a Trappist, when he had already taken simple vows, he was restless enough to tell Huvelin of his plans for setting up a community at Nazareth, living not off alms but from their own work, using a simple liturgy intelligible to uneducated local people, without property and without requirements of study. Huvelin told him to wait, and showed no enthusiasm for the project, which seems to be linked with a sermon he had once preached on the theme, 'May you so truly have taken the lowest place that no one will ever be able to take it from you.' Demanding as the Trappist rule was, the structure of the order and its rule guaranteed security, shelter and even status in comparison with the world's real out-casts, and this was the gap that brother Albéric could not accept. For him a monk in a traditional order could not be the universal brother of the poor that he wanted to be. Like many Cistercians before and since he sought a life closer to *his* view of absolute poverty, spiritual and material, and to that extent his vocation, and his conversion, did not correspond with a strictly monastic orientation.

In 1896 he drew up a form of rule for what he now called the Petits Frères de Jésus, and asked Huvelin about submitting it to Rome. Huvelin, with his customary good sense, reminded him that the rigorous poverty of St Francis' original rule had shocked the then Pope, and there would be no hope, some seven centuries later, of winning approval for a still more radical rule of poverty. Things came to a head when the Trappist authorities decided that brother Albéric should, despite his protests, proceed to ordina-tion. He was transferred from Akbès to Staouëli, just outside Algiers, in October 1896, as a base for two years theological study in Rome. By the constitutions of the order he had either to take solemn vows or leave the order by the end of January 1897, and in his perplexity he decided to leave his future in the hands of his superiors. Dom Sébastien Wyart, the Abbot-General, was a wise and humane judge of men, and on 23 January he sent for brother Albéric, then in Rome, and on his own initiative released him from the order, for which he was clearly unsuited. Henceforth Foucauld called himself brother Charles, and dropped the 'de'. He promptly took vows of perpetual poverty and chastity, but not obedience, and made for Nazareth, his spiritual home. A little more than ten years had elapsed since his conversion, and by a ceaseless process of elimination he was defining his true vocation.

Between 1897 and 1900 he worked as an odd-job man, dressed in an eccentric variant of native clothing, first for the Poor Clares at Nazareth, then for some months for the same order in Jerusa-lem, then again at Nazareth. Humble and independent though he now was, however, he was not really satisfied. In 1899 he com-posed a revised rule for his proposed fraternity, and next year, quite suddenly, events precipitated a change of direction. An abortive attempt to buy the Mount of the Beatitudes and set up a hermitage there involved financial help from his family. For this, and other reasons, he returned to Paris, and there decided, against his earlier inclination, to seek ordination. He went back to Notre-Dame-des-Neiges to prepare himself, and in June 1901 was ordained priest at Viviers, seat of the local diocese, saying his first mass at the monastery.

This meant a real break, comparable with that of his original conversion. From now on he called himself brother Charles de Jésus, and turned his back, though not ungratefully, on the inconclusive experiments of the preceding years in the Holy Land. He had decided that his true vocation was to North Africa, to the desert, where he planned to set up a *zaouia*, a kind of religious hospitality centre such as he had known during his Moroccan journey. In September 1901 he arrived in Algiers, where he was greeted by the White Father, Mgr Guérin, bishop with jurisdiction over the Sahara, and by the end of October he was at Béni-Abbès, not far from the Moroccan border in the desert. He was now quite sure that his vocation was to be a missionary, while remaining in some sense a monk, and the only outstanding problem was to define the area of his mission.

Charles began by building his modest hermitage – a tiny chapel and four small rooms – and making contacts with the varied population round about. His military training made it easy for him to win respect and affection from both officers and men, while his natural humility and linguistic gifts gave him an effective passport to the sympathies of native residents and travellers. From the first he was shocked at the effects of slavery, not only tolerated but actually protected by the French authorities, and over the years he bought the freedom of a number of slaves. To slaves in particular, but to all who sought, he gave hospitality and help. Love of God and love of neighbour, witness of Christ and a life in the service of others, such was the extent of Charles' proselytizing.

Driven on by his thirst for the absolute, and encouraged by Huvelin, he decided that the relatively civilized life at Béni-Abbès was not yet his final goal, so in 1904 he made a preliminary journey to the far south, to the Hoggar, and began an intensive study of Tamachek, the Touareg language, into which he translated the gospels. A year later, in 1905, he was pressingly invited to return south and finally accepted, to the great pleasure of his friend Laperrine, commanding the Sahara oases. The local chief, Moussa Ag Amastane, and he took to each other, eventually becoming close friends, and in August Charles had established himself at Tamanrasset, a village of some twenty families (now much larger), near the southernmost point of Algeria. Nineteen years after his conversion, fifteen years after becoming a Trappist, and only eleven before his death Charles de Foucauld, brother Charles de Jésus, had come at last to his destination.

Apart from occasional visitors he remained the only European at Tamanrasset for the next eleven years, and the immediate consequence of this was that he had no server available and was thus unable to say mass for most of the year. Only at the end of January 1908 did the Pope grant him the unusual permission to say mass alone. For a priest as devoted to the eucharist as he was, the deprivation of this Christmas mass in 1907 seemed to mark his utter isolation and the futility of all his efforts, but the Pope's action renewed his hope.

From his arrival in Tamanrasset in 1905 until his death eleven years later Charles led a life and pursued a policy which combined in an amazingly specific way all the positive elements of his life before and after his conversion. It is indeed the unique specificity of his life, and its visible fulfilment of all that went before, that gives the conversion such mystical significance. His military experience, and then his Moroccan journey, had given him a deep insight into the ways and values of the peoples of North Africa. Had he remained in the Army there can be little doubt that he would have become a colonial administrator of genius, a kind of Saharan Lyautey, a near contemporary at St-Cyr who met him again at Béni-Abbès during a tour of inspection. Soon after he arrived at Tamanrasset he drew up a programme for Moussa to improve the lot of his people, in which the main planks were education, work (especially agriculture) and family life. This typically enlightened approach, which he would no doubt have been well capable of formulating before his conversion, was, however, put in perspective by his insistence that Moussa's guiding principle should always be to know and to do God's will disinterestedly.

Again, as what would now be called a social anthropologist, he very quickly recognized that the language and culture of the Touaregs alone preserved them from complete absorption in the mixed Arab-Berber culture around them. His contact with Moussa involved a recognition of existing tribal structure and a readiness to work within it; his pioneering work on a Touareg dictionary, a list of proper names and an anthology of verse painstakingly collected from oral recitation, directly continues the intellectual enquiry instituted long before in Morocco. This time it was not study for its own sake, or even for curiosity, but with the specific aim of strengthening the racial and cultural identity of the Touaregs and thus making them easier to convert, if not to Christianity, at least to a more Christian way of life.

Similarly, the solitude and austerity he had sought with the Trappists for seven years he now practised by himself in an extreme form. He seldom went outside the small enclosure of his hermitage, partly so that those who sought him would know where to find him. His diet and daily life were comparable with those of the poor whom he had come to help, though he made no difficulty about sharing the fare offered in, for example, the officers' mess at Béni-Abbès (except on Fridays) or accepting food parcels from his anxious relatives when his health began to suffer. His timetable allowed him nearly eight hours sleep, and half an hour for all meals, compared with eleven hours work (mostly intellectual) and answering the letters which reached him in batches of twenty or thirty at a time, and five hours prayer and office.

Above all the ideal of Nazareth, of living out day by day the life of Christ with the poor, the slaves, the outcasts, permeated all he did. In practical ways, with medicine or money, food and hospitality, even toys and pictures for the children, he gave to those who had even less than he. In more specific ways too he advised Moussa, and indeed the French officers of the vast region, as to how they could best ensure the common good, but always in terms of serving God, not their own advantage. As a priest he brought the sacraments to soldiers cut off from religion for lengthy periods, and gave spiritual comfort to Christian and Moslem alike. When an aged aunt of Moussa was dying he went, at her request, to hold her hand and pray to God in her last moments. They called him Abd-Issa, servant of Jesus, but they did not see him as worshipping an alien God, rather as being a marabout, a man genuinely holy though outside Islam. Finally, as a priest, he celebrated mass (from 1908) and reserved the sacrament in a region where he, and he alone, ensured the real presence of Christ. His special devotion to the Sacred Heart (a representation of which he always wore sewn on to his *gandourah*) and his motto '*Jesus Caritas*' cannot be divorced from his daily worship before the reserved sacrament which took the place of a more formal liturgy. None of his gifts, none of his experiences was wasted in this ultimate integration of his life, but if the criterion of cost-effectiveness is to be applied the balance sheet is more problematic.

The last years raise this question of effectiveness in an acute form. In 1909 he visited France for about two months, seeing Huvelin for the last time. Next year he lost not only Huvelin but also his loyal friend Mgr Guérin (aged only 37). His new director, Father Voillard, made him agree after another visit to France in

1911 that he would go there for a few weeks every two years. In fact he went only once more, in 1913, with Ouksem, a Touareg aristocrat aged about 21, whose visit was not full of official engagements, as had been that of Moussa in 1910, but essentially a tour of Charles' relatives. War in Libya between Italy and Turkey, which began in November 1911, had repercussions across the frontier among the Saharan tribes, and famine in the area in 1912 made the usually open-handed Moussa extortionate through poverty. Charles constantly stressed the need for a permanent cadre of civilian administrators to follow up the military phase of pacification, and predicted with painful accuracy what the situation would be for the French Empire fifty years hence if this policy were not adopted.

The outbreak of war in 1914 brought a renewed threat of Senussi aggression from across the Libyan frontier. With the instinct of a soldier Charles moved his hermitage nearer the village and fortified it as a traditional *bordj* (fort) to afford some protection for local people from armed raids, actually storing weapons and ammunition within the walls. On 1 December 1916 such a raid at last took place. Betrayed by a former Touareg guest, who persuaded him to open the door, Charles was taken prisoner and left in charge of a fifteen-year-old boy with a rifle. Making some movement or sign, apparently to warn approaching tribesmen, Charles alarmed the boy, who lost his head and shot him. Technically victim of an accident rather than a martyr, brother Charles died at Tamanrasset as humbly as he had lived.

This bald recital of the events of the last years is matched by Charles' religious activity. From about 1908 he had been trying to win support for an association of lay missionaries, men and women, to live and work as farmers, teachers and the like in the Sahara, and a priest of Lyons, abbé Crozier, organized propaganda and prayers for the association, which in fact attracted as recruits and few sympathizers. Crozier's death in 1916, followed a few months later by that of Charles, seemed to mark the failure of that endeavour. It was in any case not easy to enlist support for a missionary who in fifteen years had not achieved a single conversion. The last time he wrote in detail of his own cherished plan was in 1912, to a young Trappist who was thinking of joining him. He wrote then of hermitages of three or four brothers at most, without sung office or sung liturgy, but with silent devotion before the sacrament, essentially the life of a very poor and austere family, with no detailed rules. Neither this monk, nor anyone else at any time, came to join him for more than a week or two in his active solitude. Such isolation prompts inevitable questions. In a brief biography (the first) of Charles, published in 1910, Crozier had defined the Christian life as 'pray, act, suffer' and this Charles undoubtedly did. But there is another, more puzzling, side to his life and personality. J.-F. Six writes: 'Like Jesus, his friend, brother Charles believes in friendship. This friendship is not real if it is one-way: what brother Charles seeks with all his heart is reciprocity.'[2]

His capacity for friendship is amply attested through intimates like Huvelin or General Laperrine, unknown natives or obscure monks and above all his cousin Marie de Bondy. In his relationships with all of them he gave and inspired genuine love and friendship. Numerous letters survive in which he shares his hopes and fears with others, and many are the recollections of those who treasured their meetings with him. He was the universal brother, and accepted as such, yet he remained a missionary without converts, a master without disciples, founder of an order without members. In some real sense he failed, and knew it; one must ask why. As a person he was easy to get on with, though apt to become impatient; he seems to have had no fear of rejection such as inevitably provokes rejection, but his loneliness must be seen as an essential part not merely of his human personality but of what he conceived his humble emulation of Christ to demand.

He was temperamentally unsuited to a life of obedience, and the corollary seems to be that he was not suited to command either. Moral or spiritual leadership is a very different thing, but if, for example, he had stayed in the Army, he would have done better left to his own devices in some raiding party or administering some remote region than in any conventional command structure. He always made such demands on himself as no close companion could share for more than a very short time; the rabbi who went with him on his Moroccan journey managed – just – to hold out, but not without exasperating him by his frequent failure to stand the pace set, physically and morally. Spiritually he quite simply demanded more of men than they could give, or at least more than they could give in his company. The clue is probably that never-forgotten sermon by Huvelin on keeping the last place; Charles regarded it as his by right, and it is hard to see how it could have been shared.

One begins to see that his conversion was at root a total denial of pride, an acceptance of unmerited love, a search for humility and responding love so absolute that pride and selfishness could be exorcised for ever. On the ample evidence available, he made real efforts to acccpt monastic obedience, but, as he wrote, sooner or later (he thought within two years or so) the hierarchical structure of the Trappists would have forced him to take a position of authority with others subordinate to him, and this he found incompatible with his need to be last. In another person one might speak of a compulsive quest for failure, a need to feel worthless, but this was not at all the case with Charles. His linguistic work alone would be enough to prove that while he refused all personal credit (he claimed merely to have written up the notes of his dead friend, the linguist Motylinski, who had in fact learned far more from him), he passionately cared that the job should measure up to the most exacting standards of scholarship. Nor was he indifferent to the practical and political advice he gave to Moussa and his people. Rather one should see his apparent failure in Pascal's terms as a question of orders. In the battle for men's souls, in the order of charity, who can dare to say that he failed? By identifying himself with Christ he ensured that non-Christians would recognize that his moral and spiritual qualities were the product of his faith, so that in respecting him they necessarily respected it, without thereby understanding or accepting it. Moreover, the master who died the shameful death of a felon, denied and abandoned by his closest friends, had set the example of one kind of failure for all time to those who have eyes only for what they want to see. St Teresa of Avila and St John of the Cross, two of his favourite writers, spoke to him not only of the demands of divine love, but also of the dark night which may precede and cloud it.

The sequel to Charles de Foucauld's death is so much part of his life that to omit it would be like failing to mention the *Pensées* in talking of Pascal. A strangely symbolic event was the immediate postscript. On 21 December 1916 a French officer came to Tamanrasset to investigate the circumstances of the raid and Charles' death and found his monstrance buried in the sand, containing a consecrated host. This he reverently conveyed back to his own post and administered sacramentally to one of his men, a former seminarist, three weeks after Charles had died. Then, in 1929, Charles' body was moved, against his express wishes, and reburied at the important oasis of El Goléa, more accessible than Tamanrasset. The officially sponsored biography by René Bazin (1921) had made Foucauld's name quite famous, and there was a move for his beatification. In 1933, however, there occurred something much more in accord with Charles' way of thinking than such ecclesiastical honours. René Voillaume, soon to become first superior of the Petits Frères de Jésus, came with four other young priests to El Abiodh, on the edge of the Sahara, to try and live according to the rule Charles had launched into space in 1899, and which had fired the imagination of young men who had never known him. War interrupted their experiment, essentially monastic in character at that stage, but they began again in 1945, by which time two groups of Petites Soeurs had also been formed.

At the present time Charles' disciples occupy not only his own hermitages at Béni-Abbès, Tamanrasset and Asekrem (high in the mountains some 50 kilometres from Tamanrasset and first occupied by Charles for still greater solitude in 1911), but are to be found throughout the world in small working groups of three or four, just as he had foreseen. Their houses exist in urban slums and rural poverty, from Papua to Alaska, from Venezuela to Vietnam, from Leeds to Marseilles, and everywhere they live and work with and like the poor people around them. Interestingly, the novitiate and spiritual centre to which they periodically withdraw is still in the Sahara. To an extent that he never foresaw, the many men and women who follow his example, and only began to do so seventeen years after his death, have totally vindicated his belief that the great mass of humanity can best be touched from within, in factory and field, not from without by the traditional missionary techniques of institutional churches. The demands of these various congregations of Little Brothers and Sisters are uncompromising, and though their numbers and years of existence now make them supportive to individual members, the work will always be lonely, whether in industry, on the land or at sea. It now looks as though the apparent failure of Charles de Foucauld's mission was the necessary condition for the growth of his following. 'Except the seed die . . .' The titles of René Voillaume's account of this present and lasting phase neatly sum up the twin lessons; in French it is *Au Coeur des Masses* (At the Heart of the Masses), in English *Seeds of the Desert*.

9

EDITH STEIN

The same historical events which brought about Edith Stein's death and made her, in the eyes of many, a martyr are also responsible for her comparative lack of fame today. No doubt she would not only have gone on writing, and being published, she would probably have produced work of real distinction. As it is, one must make a conscious effort to keep apart what she actually was and did from the tragic implications of her death, and from speculation as to what she would otherwise have achieved. She belongs without question with the other remarkable men and women studied in this book, and the particularity of her conversion brings into sharper focus problems faced by many converts of whom little or nothing is known.

Edith Stein was born at Breslau on 12 October 1891, by a strange concidence the date of the Day of Atonement that year. She was the youngest of seven children, and came of a numerous tribe; her father's family numbered twenty-three (by three mothers), her mother's fifteen. Both were devout Jews. Before she was three Edith lost her father, and her redoubtable mother took over the family timber business, while continuing to run the house and look after the younger children with some help from the older ones. A photograph of Frau Stein, taken in later life, shows a face of iron determination, but not without humanity. It is clear from abundant evidence that Frau Stein combined natural strength of character with a deeply religious outlook on life, not just punctilious practice.

Precocious from her earliest years, Edith was bored at kindergarten and could not wait to go on to a proper school. Her schooldays seem to have been happy and successful. After some hesitation about continuing her studies she enrolled at the University of Breslau in 1911 and was there first attracted to philosophy as a subject. Up to about this time (she specified 'from thirteen to twenty-one') she regarded herself in retrospect as an atheist, though as a matter of courtesy and convention she accompanied her mother to synagogue. It may be relevant to note that her brilliance at school seems to have occasioned some anti-semitic reactions, and one cannot rule out the possibility that in losing her early, unquestioning faith she was, in adolescence, also rebelling against racial identification. In the Kaiser's Germany, despite some discrimination and prejudice, there was nothing remotely like persecution of Jews, who indeed rose to positions of social and professional eminence, but they were a self-conscious community, and religious Jews in particular were, by definition, conformist and inward-looking.

At all events Edith was intellectually, if not spiritually, ready for a new faith, and this she found in the philosophical doctrine of phenomenology, still quite novel, evolved by Edmund Husserl (1859–1938), a Jew, like so many German philosophers of the day, of Austrian origin. His doctrine has been defined as 'a descriptive science concerned with the discovery and analysis of essences and essential meanings. It professed to exclude all metaphysical questions.'[1] In fact Husserl began from a standpoint resembling Platonic realism, and in many ways represented a return to a more traditional form of philosophy than that of the then dominant system of Hegel. He came to emphasize the actual phenomena perceived instead of purely intellectual abstractions as the source of knowledge. For some twenty years or more, up to the advent of Hitler, phenomenology was the principal philosophical school in Germany, but so many of its exponents were Jewish that Nazism virtually extinguished it. It continues, however, to excite interest in America, and through Heidegger, a pupil of Husserl, the various existentialist schools owe much to his teaching.

So fired was Edith by this new interest that when the opportunity offered of going to Göttingen, where Husserl then was, at the request of a cousin of hers whose wife lacked feminine company, she at once seized it. It was perfectly normal in Germany then to attend two or three universities in the course of one's studies. So, on 17 April 1913, Edith arrived in Göttingen on the first stage of what was to be a quite new life, though she originally planned to return to Breslau to finish her course.

At twenty-two, intelligent and industrious, she was very receptive to new influences, especially now that she was away from home. The first and greatest of these was unquestionably that of Husserl himself, an imposing figure then, in his mid-fifties, at the height of his fame. As one biographer puts it, 'she had an intense devotion for Husserl which remained with her all her life',[2] and since she is never known to have been in love or been seriously courted by any man, this devotion may well have been the strongest emotion she ever felt for any man. To say that this is a classic case of compensation for a father never known is no doubt correct, but not particularly illuminating. Husserl was at once impressed by this highly competent student, who had actually read his latest work, and always thought well of her, but their relationship was cordial rather than intimate, and quite unclouded by emotional complications.

Another new acquaintance was Adolph Reinach, Husserl's principal assistant (*Privatdozent*), a Jew, recently and happily married, who was also a good friend to her. A third was Max Scheler (1874–1928), whose mother had been Jewish but who had become a Catholic before lapsing, as a result of a marriage to a divorcée, and being received again (1916) on the breakdown of the marriage, only to lapse once more in 1922. For all his personal instability Scheler was a gifted philosopher, who developed the Platonic elements in phenomenology in an attempted defence of a Christian metaphysic, and it is a matter of record that it was he who first introduced Edith to Catholicism as a phenomenon at least worthy of note. Too little evidence has survived from this period of her life to permit of any but the most tentative conclusions regarding her attitude to religion, but it is certain that she was by now discussing it with a number of Christian friends, some of whom were recent converts from nominal Judaism.

The outbreak of war must have affected her daily life, but did not seriously interrupt her career. In January 1915 she passed the *Staatsexamen*, and after some months as a temporary Red Cross nurse went back to Göttingen to complete her thesis. A further temporary job, as a teacher in a Breslau school, was followed by her rather delayed oral examination, as a result of which she passed her doctorate *summa cum laude* in August 1916. Husserl had by now transferred to Freiburg im Breisgau, and with Reinach away in the army found himself without an assistant. Dr Edith Stein, as she now was, was offered the vacant post, and began work in October, giving an introductory course for Husserl's students and undertaking the laborious task of deciphering and transcribing the master's notes.

Edith seems to have discharged her duties very competently and contentedly, and it was natural that when Reinach was killed in November 1917 she should be sent to the funeral and entrusted with the task of putting his papers in order. Remembering the couple's deep attachment, Edith accepted the mission of condolence with the widow somewhat fearfully. In fact Frau Reinach showed such strength and serenity in her bereavement that those who came to comfort her themselves found consolation. As a recent convert to (Protestant) Christianity, Frau Reinach made it clear to all that she accepted her loss as her share of the cross, and Edith's recognition of this quite unexpected reaction added an emotional element to her already awakened interest in Christianity. She was so reserved about her inner life that the stages of her development cannot be charted, but it is hardly in doubt that her spiritual quest effectively dates from this encounter, her first realization of what the cross means to believers.

In October 1918 Husserl fell ill, and Edith helped to nurse him, and then at last the war ended. Edith went home to Breslau for a time, unsuccessfully applied (with Husserl's support) for a post at Göttingen, and then went back to Freiburg in 1919. A philosophical essay she wrote about this time rather surprisingly includes a reference to what can only be called her prayer life, and an experience, which may have been mystical, involving some kind of response to prayer. While the passage is part of a discussion of other, unrelated, psychological phenomena, the fact that it appeared at all is of obvious significance.

Meanwhile Edith had become very friendly with Hedwig Conrad-Martius, another of Husserl's pupils and, like her husband, a devout Lutheran. She often stayed with them, sometimes on their farm at Bergzabern in the Palatinate, and while on holiday there in the summer of 1921 (no more precise date is recorded) had her decisive experience. One evening she wanted something to read, and quite by chance picked up the *Life* of St Teresa of Avila (1515–82), reformer of the Carmelite Order. Despite the title this is an account, written at her confessor's request by the saint herself, of her spiritual development only up to 1562. There are a few biographical facts, but much the greater part of the forty chapters is devoted to an account of her intense prayer-life, including the so-called prayer of union, and her ecstasies, in which the person of Christ, especially in the garden of Gethsemane and on the cross, is invariably central. St Teresa was quite without intellectual training, and what she writes belongs solely to the spiritual dimension, expressed in terms of the utmost devotional fervour.

Edith read the book right through and at the end said to herself 'this is the truth'.[3] From that moment she resolved to seek Catholic baptism and become a Carmelite. In an account of her vocation written in December 1938 Edith specifically says that this book 'brought to an end my long search for the true faith'.

Her next act was characteristic: she went next day to buy a catechism and a missal, began attending mass at Bergzabern, and when she was satisfied that she had mastered the contents of these two essential books applied to the astonished local priest for baptism. Although she had received no formal instruction in the faith she had no trouble convincing him that she was ready.

On 1 January 1922 Edith was baptized, and also received communion. By special dispensation her friend Hedwig, though not a Catholic, acted as sponsor. A month later she was confirmed. In the account of her conversation just quoted she goes on to say: 'When I received Holy Baptism I thought this was but a preparation for entering the Order [Carmelite]'[4], but she under-estimated the obstacles still across her path. Conversion had set her on the road, shown her the goal, but had not yet made it accessible.

The first and much the hardest task was to tell her mother. Soon after her confirmation she went home and broke the news. Her mother, and most of her family, took it very hard, trying to explain it away by such stock excuses as an unhappy love affair. Edith felt this inner separation very keenly, but commented 'such sorrow is also very fruitful'.[5] More to the point, it became ineluctably evident that she could not pursue her chosen path to Carmel (as Carmelites describe their vocation). She wrote 'she [mother] would not die of it, but it would fill her with a bitterness for which I could not be responsible'.[6] This was also the view of her spiritual director, Canon Schwindt of Speyer, an experienced, elderly priest with a wide reputation as a wise director. Quite apart from the problem of her mother's reaction, he, and others, were insistent that Edith's outstanding intellectual gifts should continue to be used, in teaching as before, but now in a specifically Catholic context. No one supported her desire to become a Carmelite.

The next stage of her spiritual journey must in most ways have been the most difficult. Family tensions and the frustration of her vocation were only partly compensated by a job teaching in a school for which, as a former university lecturer, she was not really suited. She went to live in a convent of Dominican Tertiary nuns who ran a large girls' school at Speyer, and as far as circumstances permitted lived the life of a religious, spending long hours in silent prayer in the chapel as well as attending the regular services. She seems to have made quite a good impression on her pupils and the nuns, but people found her rather stiff and unapproachable. Her physical posture reflected this attitude; she always spoke in a low voice, without gestures, would kneel bolt upright for hours on end in the chapel and made no more allowance for the frailty of others than her own, so that she could be sometimes wounding and harsh. A good comment on this phase of her life is this: 'She had given herself wholly to God, but she had not yet reached the fullness of charity where every strain is released.'[7]

In 1927 Canon Schwindt died, and she went for the first time at Easter 1928 to the great Benedictine abbey of Beuron, where she at once felt at home. The abbot, Dom Walzer, agreed to replace Schwindt as her director, but he too insisted that she should go on with her intellectual apostolate rather than try a religious vocation. She was becoming well known in Catholic intellectual circles through writing and lecturing at conferences, and, always an ardent feminist, she was much in demand as a lecturer to Catholic women's organizations. She had also, in 1925, translated two volumes of Newman's letters and journals into German at the invitation of a scholarly Jesuit, and went on to translate some of St Thomas Aquinas. This she found strange and hard to grasp, never having met scholasticism before, but when in 1929 Heidegger organized a volume in tribute to Husserl's seventieth birthday, Edith contributed an essay, originally in dialogue form, attempting to reconcile the philosophies of Aquinas and Husserl. Thenceforth her philosophical thinking ran very much on those lines, and while she never overcame her lack of scholastic training, there is every indication that she was on the way to making an original and fruitful synthesis between two apparently antagonistic systems.

In 1931 she began to realize that her real future lay in higher rather than secondary education, so she went to Freiburg to see the now very eminent Heidegger about the prospects of a post. After some discussion she finally, in 1932, accepted the offer of a post at Münster, at the Institute of Education, and took up residence in a Catholic college for student teachers, mostly nuns. There she continued to lead a life as near as possible to that of a religious. After addressing a Catholic conference at Aachen in October she wrote the revealing words: 'I realize only now . . . how utterly alien the world had become to me, and how much it costs me to make contact with it. I do not think I can ever quite succeed in doing so again.'[8] By now her sister Rosa wanted to become Christian, but reluctantly agreed for the sake of her mother to defer any decisive step, and to keep her intentions secret. As the Nazis inexorably made their way to power Edith remained deeply conscious of her Jewishness, and her last public lecture, in 1933, was in fact on Nazism and race.

Edith's personal anguish was now compounded by public menace. Her relations with her mother and other members of her family were cordial, but they inevitably saw her as someone who had denied what they stood for. She herself naturally saw her new faith as the complement and fulfilment of her old. At the same time the strident racism of the Nazis took no account of creed in its obsession with blood as the only criterion of human worth. Faithful or faithless, converts or crypto-Jews, all lived under the same threat. Solidarity seemed to demand closing the ranks, not defections, and as the crisis intensified Edith's dilemma became daily more painful.

1933 came, and with the new year catastrophe. In January Hitler became Chancellor; in March, after the Reichstag fire, the Nazis became the strongest party and Hitler was granted plenary powers for five years. Although he was not proclaimed Reichsführer until August 1934, following the death of President Hindenburg, Hitler and his men ruled every aspect of German life from 1933. For far too long far too many Germans, including Jews, could not believe that he intended to do exactly as he had said, and those who had no doubts on that score were all too often classed with the neurotic alarmists who always cry wolf at every change of régime. Edith was under no illusions; indeed, she was so concerned that she wrote a personal letter to Pope Pius XI, and entrusted it to Abbot Walzer when she learned that she had no chance of a private audience. She begged the Pope to make some statement about the Jewish question, but of course Vatican policy towards the new German government was not to be decided on such a simple view of right and wrong.

By the end of April the terrifyingly rapid spread of Nazi control made her job at Münster impossible, and indeed threatened the whole future of independent religious education. The main objection long held to Edith's Carmelite vocation had ceased once her intellectual apostolate became blocked, and there seems no doubt that this is how she saw the interruption of a career she had always regarded as second best. On 30 April 1933, Good Shepherd Sunday (so-called after the gospel for the day), she went to the church of St Ludger in Münster where a special service of ten hours' continuous devotion was going on, and resolved not to leave until she knew whether or not it was God's will that she should enter Carmel. She remained praying to the end and then recorded: 'When the final benediction had been given I had the consent of the Good Shepherd.'[9]

Thereafter events moved with great speed. She had to await Abbot Walzer's return from Rome, but after a few days she had his consent. She was then interviewed by the priest in charge of the Cologne Carmel, and later by the whole community, who asked her to sing a little song (a custom of the house) while they inspected her from behind the grille of the enclosure. Next day the nuns voted in chapter to accept her, despite her age, and as soon as she received their telegram in Münster began preparations for the move. With a formalism typical of her she arranged to celebrate the patronal feast of Our Lady of Mount Carmel (16 July) at Cologne and then spent a month with the extern sisters outside the actual enclosure. There was no going back, but the worst part of the journey lay ahead, as she knew all too well.

In September she went home as usual, and was at first evasive about her plans, but after a week or two at last broke the news to her mother, who was inconsolable. Quite by chance the Cologne Carmel was setting up a new foundation in Breslau at just this time, and one of the two sisters sent for this purpose came several times to see Frau Stein and try to win her over, but in vain. Edith herself wrote five years later: 'The decision was so difficult that no one could say with certainty whether this road or that was the right one. Good reasons could be advanced for either. I had to take the step entirely in the darkness of faith.'[10] Only now, after twelve years, was the original conversion experience complete, but in circumstances so tragically different that no one could even have imagined them in 1921.

Her last day at home was her birthday, 12 October, which happened to coincide with the Jewish Feast of Tabernacles that year. She accompanied her mother to synagogue, and at the old lady's insistence (Frau Stein was eighty-four) walked home, some three-quarters of an hour, for more opportunity to talk. When the birthday guests had gone Edith for the first and last time in her life helped her mother undress for bed. The finality of their parting, physical and emotional, was beyond question the hardest sacrifice Edith had to make. Next day, early in the morning, she left for Cologne and on 14 October, the feast of St Teresa (another touch of formalism) Edith Stein at last entered the enclosure of Carmel.

The prioress recalled later that at their first meeting Edith had said: 'Human activity cannot help us, but only the passion of Christ . . . my desire is to share in that.'[11] From the first, from her illumination of 1921, Edith had known that Carmel meant renouncing her intellectual gifts, but by 1933 she saw her sacrifice in more sombre terms, 'to be a victim of expiation in the name of Israel'. It would be a mistake to see her final step as prompted primarily by a consideration which only became real in 1933, but it would equally be a mistake to overlook the new and tragic element in a vocation which she had believed in despite constant discouragement for all those years. In the light of the actual moment of decision, her parting from her mother, and the bitterness she had to bear on that account, was not an auspicious beginning for her religious life.

She passed the period of probation, and on 15 April 1934 gave up even her name, being clothed solemnly (that is, received into the order as a novice) under the name of Sister Teresa Benedicta of the Cross, a compliment to the Benedictine Abbot Walzer who officiated at the ceremony and who had made Beuron her spiritual home until she entered Carmel. If the persistence of her Carmelite vocation was some guarantee of its authenticity, there were many practical reasons why she found real difficulty in adapting to the new life, for all the inner serenity it brought her. The community was small, limited to twenty-one, and the other novices some twenty years her junior. They had no intellectual training or activity, and it was not hard for Edith to be modest about an academic distinction of which none of them had heard. Apart from the services in chapel and private prayer, most of their day was taken up with the most humdrum domestic chores. When the entry of the new sister was announced it seems that the first question asked about her was whether she could sew (she could not).

There is nothing very heroic about such a modest and well-ordered, sheltered life, and yet it makes emotional and spiritual demands on those who follow it which lead to real heroism – for example in the Spanish Civil War and in the French Revolution. For twelve years Edith had been imposing on herself all kinds of burdens, neither eating nor sleeping adequately, kneeling rigidly in prayer for hours, making no concession to her own or others' weakness. Now, and for the rest of her life, she lived under obedience, forced to subordinate her own will, even for austerity, to the wisdom, or simply the custom, of others much more ordinary than she was. Her previous excessive rigour must in some measure have been linked with her upbringing and then her break with ancestral Judaism, certainly an attempt to justify her conversion by driving herself to the limit of endurance, perhaps a covert form of spiritual pride. Now, 'under the rule of obedience which, while cutting at the roots of self-love, took full account of the limitations of their physical endurance, Edith Stein was gradually freed from a weakness whose very existence she had evidently never suspected when she was in the world.'[12] The outward signs of the change were a more relaxed, according to one witness, 'more maternal' attitude replacing the earlier rigidity and reserve. Her conversion was at last fulfilled and making her what she had not been free to be before.

In April 1935 she was professed; that is, took vows for five years in the first instance, and explicitly told a friend that, far from being safe in Carmel, she was going to suffer for her people and 'that she was going to bring many home'.[13] About this time her mother at last began to answer the letters Edith had faithfully been sending every week, and an element in this partial reconciliation must have been Edith's steadfast refusal to renounce her own people in this time of growing persecution. When in September 1936 her mother died, aged eighty-seven, the worst of the bitterness had gone. An immediate consequence of her mother's death was that Rosa came to Cologne and was baptized in Edith's presence on Christmas Eve. Eighteeen months later, in April 1938, Husserl died, dismissed from teaching as a non-Aryan and nursed by a former pupil who had become a Benedictine nun.

At the orders of her superiors Edith had continued work on her book attempting to reconcile Thomism and phenomenology, under the title *Endliches und Ewiges Sein* (*Finite and Eternal Being*), but having already had reviews and articles returned by publishers afraid to accept work from non-Aryans, she had little hope of seeing her book in print. By 1938 she had found a publisher, and had actually received some proofs, before it became clear that the book would never appear, at least in Germany, under her own name, and she was not prepared to resort to subterfuge to get it published. It was in fact published with other of her works after the war. The completion of this work did, however, free her for other study, and she became deeply interested in St John of the Cross, with St Teresa the spiritual father of the reformed Carmelite tradition and one of the greatest of mystical theologians.

Meanwhile the world outside Carmel was coming ever closer to the abyss. In connection with various elections the local Gestapo had already noted the presence of Dr Edith Stein, disqualified as a Jewess from voting. On 9 November 1938 came the infamous *Kristallnacht*, when Jews, their property and syngagogues all over Germany were systematically attacked and destroyed by Nazi gangsters. It was no longer possible for Edith to remain in Cologne without endangering the other nuns, so on New Year's Eve she was driven to safety at Echt not far across the border in Dutch Limburg, where once before, in face of Bismarck's persecution, the Cologne Carmel had sought refuge, and which maintained a tradition of recruiting German nuns.

For the moment she seemed out of danger. She was no longer young, and found it hard to settle down in another small community, rather stricter than in Cologne and with different customs, but she made the effort, and even learned Dutch, unlike some of the other Germans, the better to fit in with local ways. After some vicissitudes Rosa eventually came to join her (not as a nun) in the summer of 1940. So far as one can judge Edith went on leading a normal Carmelite life, busy with household chores, reading what few books she could get hold of and composing a work on mystical theology, based on St John of the Cross, called *Kreuzeswissenschaft* (*Science of the Cross*), and left uncompleted, but rescued from destruction against all probability by the nuns, and later published.

The invasion of Holland in 1940, and subsequent German occupation, led inevitably to interviews with the Gestapo, first in Maastricht nearby, then in Amsterdam, and the extreme danger in which she and Rosa found themselves became only too evident. By 1941 negotiations had begun for them both to be accepted by Carmelites in Switzerland. Endless procedural difficulties caused delay, and in retrospect the lack of urgency with which such requests for asylum were treated seems amazing. It must be remembered that even by the end of the war few Germans other than those undeniably implicated would admit to knowing the facts of the dreadful 'Final Solution', and individuals and governments outside Germany who may have suspected, or even known for certain from secret sources, what was going on, found it expedient to concentrate on other priorities. The Swiss in particular were so geographically vulnerable that they had to act with the greatest caution lest in saving a relatively small number of refugees they might expose themselves (and the refugees) to savage reprisal.

At all events Edith, like everyone else, knew about concentration camps and deportation of Jews and others to Eastern Europe. She knew that no one ever came back, but one cannot be sure that in 1941 or 1942 the official policy of mass extermination had yet been fully realized by the victims. Whether it had or not, Edith showed complete indifference to her own fate, but co-operated fully in the attempts to secure asylum in Switzerland; she was not seeking death, but she was prepared for it.

In July 1942 the religious authorities in Holland, including the Catholic bishops, issued a public protest against Nazi treatment of Dutch Jews, especially those converts who were separated from their Christian communities. The response of the occupant was typically swift and brutal. All over Holland Jews were arrested on 2 August and taken to transit camps in readiness for deportation. Edith and Rosa were given ten minutes to pack, and then driven to the camp at Westerbork in Eastern Holland. For a day or two Dutch friends were allowed contact, and there are reports of Edith, still in her habit, trying to comfort others, especially mothers and children, in the camp.

Her last message to the Carmel at Echt asks for items of clothing and speaks of her continuing opportunity for prayer. The details of the end remain obscure, and may never be known for certain, but it seems that the Dutch Jews were taken by train to Auschwitz in a succession of transports from about 6 or 7 August 1942, and that Edith was probably killed there with her sister on 9 August 1942, like tens of thousands of others, just for being a Jew.

Neither she nor any of the others had any choice. There was nothing they could do or say to undo the fact of their race once physical flight had become impossible, and they did not die for bearing witness to their faith, Christian or Jewish, though at the end we hear of many such instances of heroic witness. They were all martyrs of man's appalling inhumanity to man, but it does them no service to think of them as religious martyrs. Edith, and probably other Christian Jews, had, however, prayed long before, already in 1935, that she might offer herself to suffer for her people, and in the early years she could easily have left Germany. She did not stay from inertia, or false optimism, but determined to share the cross laid on her people. She had to that extent chosen in advance to accept, if not actively to provoke, a kind of martyrdom, and it would be right to see this choice as an integral part, a logical consequence of her conversion. It would, however, be totally wrong to assess the quality of that conversion by the manner of her death. Even if she had died of natural causes before the Gestapo came for her, it was her life in Carmel, what she accepted and what she renounced, her living reconciliation of the Old with the New Covenant that made her what she was. That last night with her mother in Breslau tells us more about Edith Stein than the sordid horror of Auschwitz.

10

SIMONE WEIL

Simone Weil inevitably invites comparison with Edith Stein; both were of Jewish parentage, both became teachers of philosophy, both moved from agnosticism to acknowledge the call of Christ. There, however, the resemblance stops. Apparent points of comparison with other converts prove on investigation to be equally misleading. Simone Weil defies classification, and it is typical of her uniqueness that the inner life for which she is now known was quite unsuspected even by her devoted brother until after her death. She alone of all those studied in this book refused baptism, no doubt perversely, but because, not in spite of, her conversion. She belongs unquestionably to the number of those who have been called; no one can tell whether she was also chosen.

Simone Weil was born in Paris in 1909 to parents of Jewish stock but no religious persuasion. She seems to have been on affectionate terms with her parents and elder brother, André, but a childhood acquaintance recalls that Simone did not like being kissed, nor did she have any dolls or toys. It may be relevant that the war, in which her father served as an Army doctor, cut across her early years, and that such altruistic acts as saving sugar for sending to soldiers and adopting one to whom letters and parcels were sent formed part of her childhood experience.

After the war she had an apparently uneventful education at various schools, ending up in 1925 at the Lycée Henri IV, near the Sorbonne, under the famous philosophy teacher Alain (Emile Chartier). Simone Pétrement, her biographer and a friend already in those early days, ascribes great importance to Alain's influence on Simone Weil's habits of mind, in particular her great emphasis on the role of attention in finding truth, that is, clearing the mind with a conscious effort in readiness to receive whatever may enter. From this time on she acquired a considerable facility for writing essays on a variety of philosophical subjects, and some of them have been preserved.

From Henri IV she went on in 1925 to the Ecole Normale in the rue d'Ulm nearby, the only girl of her year at this peculiarly French establishment for the young intellectual élite. After writing a diploma dissertation on Descartes she passed out as an *agrégée de philosophie* (that is, she passed a competitive examination entitling her to a post teaching the senior form in a *lycée*) in 1931. During this period she became closely involved in political activity on the left wing, especially with the trade union movement (CGT), and was nicknamed by one of her disapproving professors 'the Red Virgin'. The fact of belonging to an élite, chosen by competition, distinguished in quality, quantity and physical location from the mass of Paris students, imparts to *normaliens* a feeling of innate superiority seldom tempered by humility, and in both a positive and a negative way intense awareness of intellectual pride, and its dangers, became an outstanding feature of Simone Weil's character.

She began her teaching career in 1931 at le Puy, making a name for herself locally by becoming involved in demonstrations by the unemployed workers in the town, whose desperate plight she brought to the notice of the municipal authorities with more force than tact. At the industrial centre of St-Etienne, not far away, she made friends with a number of trade union militants, and altogether lived up to her nickname of Red Virgin.

Transferred a year later to Auxerre she continued much the same line of conduct, and in the interval between the two posts visited Germany, where she saw the Nazis preparing to take over and made contact with various left-wing elements.

In 1933 she was moved again, this time to Roanne, nearer her friends at St-Etienne. On the last day of that year she spent the evening at her parent's home in Paris with Trotsky. She was, to say the least, not overawed. Despite her vigorous political and union activity she seems to have won personal respect as a teacher, and real affection from some of her girl pupils, but it is by no means clear that she would have made a successful career over any long period. Her way of life was already markedly eccentric; she took no trouble over material needs like food or lodging, she dressed with conspicuous lack of elegance, and she showed no regard for social conventions, preferring to frequent working-class cafés rather than the sort of bourgeois establishment favoured by her colleagues. Her passionate commitment to the cause of social justice cannot be doubted, and what might be exhibitionism in someone else seems to have been a spontaneous reaction in her. Spontaneity, of course, is quite consistent with silliness, or even absurdity, and is then only enhanced by intellectual brilliance.

In these terms the *reductio ad absurdum* of Simone Weil's social principles came in 1934, when she took leave from teaching in order to experience factory work at first hand. Being the person she was, nothing less than the most exacting manual labour would do. She was already subject to crippling headaches (never satisfactorily diagnosed), and the utterly unsuitable work she forced herself to do further undermined her health. Less than two months after beginning work an ear infection obliged her to take several weeks off (partly in Switzerland, at her parents' insistence), and on her return to work she was laid off again after no more than two weeks. In the end she decided to leave the factory, having worked there from December 1934 to April 1935, with interruptions amounting to some four weeks in all.

She had secured her first job through an acquaintance; next time she resolved to get work herself. She succeeded, but in a job so completely unsuitable (at a stamping press) that she lasted less than a month. Finally, she was hired by Renault and, with some days off due to minor injury, stayed there from June until late August. Her own comment on this series of experiences was 'contact with affliction had killed my youth' and gave her the 'first feeling of the religion of the slaves'. She seems thereafter to have been more subdued, less prone to violent anger and physically much debilitated.

At least she no longer had any illusions about the facts of working life, but she never abandoned her obstinate conviction that neither her physique nor her intellectual training disqualified her from sharing it with the slaves. One apparently direct consequence of the factory experience was 'the first of three contacts with Christianity that have really counted'[1] – the sight of some poor women in a Portuguese fishing village going in procession round the ships for some patronal festival. The wretchedness of the people, together with her own physical wretchedness, brought home to her that 'Christianity is pre-eminently the religion of slaves'.[2]

She spent the school year 1935–6 at a *lycée* in Bourges, but then in August embarked on another episode of serio-comic absurdity. The Spanish Civil War attracted her, like so many other left-wing intellectuals; she duly made her way to Spain and enlisted on the

Republican side. After less than a month of somewhat erratic
active service, her military career came abruptly and ingloriously
to an end when she stumbled over a pan of boiling oil and suffered
severe burns. Her parents came to rescue her – one is irresistibly
reminded of some problem child at boarding school – and by late
September she was back in Paris, heavily engaged in the Popular
Front (the movement led by Léon Blum).

In March 1937 she decided to go to Italy, which she loved, and
in Assisi she had, as she records, the second of her decisive
contacts with Christianity. This time it took the form of an inner
compulsion to get down on her knees, for the first time in her life,
before the altar in St Francis' humble chapel. Art and music
delighted her during the visit, and her recent exploits in Spain
caused her no embarrassment even with dedicated Fascists. In
October she resumed her teaching career, at St-Quentin, but by
January her headaches had become so bad that she had to apply
for sick leave, and never in fact came back to teaching.

The exact course of inner development during 1938 is not too
easy to determine. Despite incessant headaches she spent ten days
over Easter at Solesmes, and missed none of the Holy Week
services. The Gregorian chant made a profound impression on
her, and it seems clear that she was in some real sense a participant
rather than a mere spectator in the services. While there she met
a young Englishman who introduced her to English religious
poetry, in particular George Herbert's beautiful poem 'Love',
which she copied out as a kind of talisman. In May she went back
to Italy, to Florence and Venice, returning to Paris in September.
Either at Solesmes or, as seems more likely, in Paris later in the
year she had the third and most important of her contacts with
Christianity.

While reading the poem 'Love' as a prayer, a habit she formed
soon after the meeting at Solesmes, she felt herself possessed by
Christ: 'In this sudden possession of me by Christ, neither my
senses nor my imagination had any part; I only felt in the midst
of my suffering the presence of love, like that which one can read
in the smile of a beloved face.'[3] At that time, she adds, she had
not yet read any mystical writers, and though totally unprepared
for this strange experience, never doubted its reality. If one goes
on to ask what actually happened, there can evidently be no
objective answer, and in this case no very revealing subjective
one either, short of having an apparently similar experience oneself. Simone Pétrement comments: 'She was not yet a believer,
but perhaps there had already occurred a certain change in her

philosophical ideas. Alain's philosophy was voluntarist in nature, the philosophy of mysticism is the exact opposite of voluntarism.'[4]

Not until 1942, three and a half years later, did she record this experience (and then only in private letters to Père Perrin and Joë Bousquet), with the benefit of hindsight, but if by then she herself thought it had been decisive, her opinion must surely be accepted.

The remaining years of her brief life were inevitably overshadowed by the harsh facts of war and enforced exile. In the summer of 1940, after the fall of France, she made her way with her parents to Marseilles, in the unoccupied zone, with the idea of eventually getting on a boat to join her brother in America. She there met Père Perrin, a Dominican who became her confidant and guide, and through him Gustave Thibon, a writer who had a farm in the Ardèche. In 1941, in August, she went to stay with Thibon at St-Marcel, and soon became an intimate friend. Once more, precarious health did not deter her from working at the grape harvest. In May 1942 she left for America, entrusting to Perrin and Thibon some of the voluminous notebooks she had been filling, and as a sort of testament wrote the two letters (to Perrin and Bousquet) already quoted.

The voyage took several weeks, and then she spent some months in New York before at last succeeding, in November 1942, in joining her Free French compatriots in London. Even now she was feverishly trying to persuade various authorities to adopt a particularly impractical scheme for recruiting a virtual suicide squad of front-line nurses, and in an even wilder flight of fancy she tried to have herself sent on a Resistance mission to France. These last years are full of letters, often never sent, to all kinds of very busy people; she obviously had a compulsion to put pen to paper. As if this were not bad enough, she had made a vow 'I will not eat more than in Marseilles', which she probably kept to the letter, because there was no one to release her from it. At all events, by spring 1943 she was so ill that she had to accept being sent to hospital, where advanced tuberculosis was diagnosed. If all are agreed that she ate as little as possible, it is not clear whether she was physically capable of eating properly, or whether long and imprudent abstinence had reduced her to a condition in which she could not have eaten more even if she had wanted to. Simone Pétrement writes: 'Did she want to die? It is hard to believe that she did not realize the danger to which she was exposing herself by eating so little.'[5] In August she was transferred from the Middlesex Hospital in London to a sanatorium in Ashford, Kent, and there she died on 24 August 1943, aged 34.

The coroner provided a legal postscript by finding: 'Suicide by refusing to eat whilst the balance of her mind was disturbed'. His is not the only verdict on her which strikes the conscientious enquirer as being non-proven.

The reasons for including Simone among those studies are all to be found in the last five years of her life, following her mystic encounter with Christ, but the nature and location of the evidence imposes the greatest caution on anyone seeking to judge her spirituality. Writing in 1960, M.-M.Davy says: 'This Jewish girl, brought up as an agnostic, had, like Pascal, received the indelible mark of a spiritual experience. Everything prepared her for it and it would be wrong in her case to speak of any kind of conversion.'[6] In 1970, on just the same point, F. de Hautefeuille (who knew Perrin but not Simone Weil) writes: 'To find the story of Simone Weil's conversion, the main, and virtually the only, source is the letter she wrote to Père Perrin' (substantially duplicated by the one to Bousquet).[7] The same writer perhaps inevitably compares her with Pascal, but comments: ' "she tasted love" but cannot even find rest in any certainity.' As for Perrin himself, the problem appears in a new light, that of the discrepancy between the objective criteria of a trained theologian and priest and the subjective criteria of Simone herself. In 1967 he writes: 'When Simone Weil came to see me in June 1941, she defined her position to me as "on the threshold of the Church", as near as one can be while remaining outside. This, on her part, was a real illusion. She was very far from Christianity . . .'[8] But if this dispassionate judgment compels respect, we must also believe Perrin's categorical assertion that only he and Bousquet knew of 'the great light which changed her life',[9] unsuspected by even her intimate friends and unrecorded in her notebooks. He adds that even Thibon knew nothing of her 'discovery' of prayer, also unreported in the notebooks. He concludes quite plainly: 'I do not see how one could doubt the supernatural character of the illumination which changed the orientation of her thought, and how one can honestly refuse her witness on God and his Christ. For her it was a certainty which never wavered, which was never in any way obscured.'[10]

As usual, much of the discordance – and concordance – between these opinions involves points of definition. It is very striking that all accept without question the fact, and authenticity, of Simone's spiritual experience. Davy's denial of conversion is directly contrary to the testimony of everyone else, including Simone Weil, and seems to derive from too rigorous an insistence on the element of novelty (rather than affirmation) in the phenomenon of conversion. Simone's own special use of the word 'orientation' very well describes the new direction taken by her thought after the decisive spiritual experience, and comes out clearly from de Hautefeuille's paraphrase: 'Thus attention, like love, which normally accompanies it, is an orientation.'[11] As for her religion, she never claimed to be a Catholic, and Perrin denies that she was even Christian at their first meeting, but de Hautefeuille puts it rather well in coining the term 'panchristism'[12] to denote her position (everything that is true is Christian) in preference to syncretism. All are unanimous that Christ was the central reality in her life after the conversion. What is harder to define is the central reality of her life before that experience.

Certain strands in her development can be discerned from the start. She was the complete intellectual, in the most intense French manner, very awkward physically, hopelessly unpractical, endlessly argumentative, and like so many other affluent bourgeois intellectuals desperately anxious to erase the guilt of her privileged class by activity on behalf of the workers. She was almost a caricature of the mad inventor with a solution for all social ills, even a more effective way of performing the factory tasks for which intellect was the last requisite. Her use, and abuse, of the power of reason led to far more absurdities than did her emotional excesses.

On the affective side the strands soon become entangled with the intellectual ones. Quite instinctively, as a child, she showed concern for anyone less fortunate than herself, and by the time she reached Ecole Normale had become a passionate supporter of campaigns to relieve famine in China or destitution somewhere else. Her militancy in politics and trade union affairs may well be a rationalization of a very early and powerful instinct.

Again on the affective side, her attitude to human relationships and emotions (somewhat reminiscent of Pascal) was fiercely individualistic and intransigently opposed to any form of self-gratification. She expected, even invited, rejection to an almost frightening degree, but at the same time her need and capacity for friendship were enormous, and some of her most memorable passages concern love and friendship. She proudly writes to and about her working-class friends as comrades, and her reckless generosity as much as her intellectual gifts (and her patience in sharing them) give reality to what would otherwise be a rather pathetic illusion. There is always a pathetic, sometimes a grotesque, aspect to her activities – her brief military career in Spain cannot have ended too soon for her apprehensive comrades in arms, and her clumsiness in factory and field was only equalled by her determination to complete an impossible self-imposed task. She exasperated no one more than her friends, and her insistence on being treated worse than anyone else must have been a sore trial to them. Lonely she certainly was, but if in any real sense she was starved of affection it was largely by her own choice.

A final ingredient in her character was an intense awareness of self; in one form this showed as intellectual pride, in another as a degree of abnegation which, in its deliberate singularity, reflects a mirror-image of that pride. This same quality led her to frequent disputes with authority – her teachers, her superiors, the officials of the Communist party and the unions and, eventually, the Church and its representatives. She found it hard to conceive that her inspiration could be wrong, or that her personal unimportance could fail to be itself important. Thibon has a brilliant sentence on this, referring to the time after her conversion but equally valid before: 'Detached in her innermost being from her own tastes and needs, she was not detached from her detachment . . . In the great book of the universe set before her eyes her ego was like a word which she had perhaps succeeded in *erasing*, but which remained *underlined*.'[13]

In such a complex character no simple formula is likely to explain major changes, but if the factory year (actually more like half a year) can be accepted as marking a turning point, part of the explanation of what followed may lie in the nature of that turning point. Excessive physical strain, and consequently impaired health, is one factor in the 'killing of her youth'; the discovery that the body, and the will, have their limits is the natural penalty of age, but a shock to youth. Similarly the realization that she, with all her advantages, was not strong or skilful enough to keep up with the underfed, underpaid, uneducated masses of the labour force must have come as a shock. Even more of a shock must have been the realization that the wage-slaves were too browbeaten to form the ranks of a liberating army of the Left, while the hard-line Communist bosses were no more interested in human dignity and freedom than the capitalist oppressors. Although Simone Weil remained to the end of her life a champion of the oppressed workers, the available solutions for their plight, even the Popular Front, lost their credibility. Never committed ideologically, she was wholly committed in idealism, and it would perhaps be inappropriate to speak in her case of 'the God who failed' of Left-wing orthodoxy; the bitterness of her defeat seems rather to have stemmed from the failure of reality to conform with intellectually based ideals.

If one goes on from such considerations to more purely affective and spiritual ones, the way to Christianity is marked by two features of Simone Weil's character and evolution; her consuming need for love and her self-identification with the 'slaves', whom love alone could redeem. She felt herself unloved, and unlovable, whatever her friends might say, and it was only a step to link such emotional deprivation with the social, economic and also emotional deprivation of the slave. It is no accident that the first of her decisive encounters with Christianity should, a few weeks after the factory, involve the Portuguese women, united in poverty and piety, and that the second, in 1937, should have been in St Francis' chapel at Assisi, where, alone, she felt forced to her knees. Still less of an accident is the personal revelation of Christ, in love, as she was praying the poem 'Love'. These experiences corresponded with her deepest needs, and led her to the religion of which they were the manifestations.

It is probably because these contacts were unbidden that she takes such a very different line from Pascal. Denying the validity of his well-known 'You would not be looking for me if you had not found me', she writes,[14] 'It is not for man to seek, nor even believe in God, he must simply refuse his love to everything other than God,' and even more emphatically: 'He who seeks hinders the operation of God more than he helps it.' This seems to suggest that when she first became aware of Christianity in a way that counted it was as a result of an experience registering in a spiritual void. A phrase written in her last year may well apply to her conversion: 'God's secret word of love cannot be anything but silence, Christ is the silence of God.'[15] It seems to follow that before Christ came into her life it was full of clamour, intellectual and emotional, with neither sense nor purpose. Afterwards he was the centre of a pattern described as 'gravity and grace' (*la pesanteur et la grâce*), and the purpose of life became '*l'attente de Dieu*' (intently waiting on God). In her view we must wait for God to come down to us, being incapable of ascent ourselves, and our proper contribution is to remain *en attente* if we love him enough. This combination of love and waiting intently is the best way to escape from the *moi* which, as in Pascal, is always hateful. In her own peculiar terminology grace is the love of God, and gravity is the necessity of the natural order, which must be obeyed if it is faithfully to reflect the love of its creator.

Between the meeting with Christ and her first serious talks with

Perrin, some eighteen months later, one must suppose that she had evolved along the lines set down in the notebooks of the last years. She had formed a special attachment to the eucharist, though she could not, of course, in those pre-Vatican II days receive the sacrament. She thought and read much about religion, expressed in part through Catholic liturgy and sacraments, though not exclusively so, and the only further step she could have taken would have been to accept baptism, and with it membership of the church and obedience to its doctrines. The combined evidence of Perrin, Thibon, the notebooks and other documents of the final three years show the distance she covered under Perrin's direction, but also the stumbling blocks she set up in her own path. In Perrin's phrase (borrowed apparently from the life of some saint) Simone was like the bell that calls people to church without itself ever going inside.

The notebooks of these years (from which translated extracts have been published as *Gravity and Grace* and *Waiting on God*) show a bewildering profusion of interests, analogies, historical and linguistic speculation, ranging from Plato and Greek drama to Sanskrit and Egyptian, but including passages of arresting insight on God and man. Such omnivorous curiosity accounts in part for her inability to accept the monopoly (as she saw it) claimed by Catholicism. Perrin considered her total lack of historical objectivity to be her chief intellectual defect. With her violent antipathy to the Jews of the Old Testament and the legacy of Imperial Rome it is hardly surprising that her view of Christianity was as biased as her view, for example, of Hinduism. Her intellectual confusion led her to accumulate objections to Christianity and Catholicism based on countless misunderstandings of fact, and sustained with obstinate perversity (her emotional support for the mediaeval Cathars, about whom she knew very little, is an example of uncritical favour shown to any anti-establishment movement), but Thibon maintains that it was immaturity, not pride, that made her behave like this. He goes on to make a distinction which explains rather than invalidates her conversion, and writes: 'Simone Weil lived almost to the point of torment the discrepancy between her message and her person. And that no doubt is where we find the nub of the contrast . . . between a painful humility . . . and intransigent assurance, fierce obstinacy',[16] not to mention amazing psychological naiveté. The only remedy for such defects is the patient assistance of wise and trusted friends, but the force of wartime circumstances and her own character deprived her of such assistance over a sufficiently long period to be effective.

She seemed quite incapable of considering that her obsessive insistence on humility might itself be a form of pride, and even if Thibon is correct in attributing it simply to immaturity, her criteria appear dangerously absolute. An extraordinary sentence rationalizes what looks suspiciously like a psychological disposition. Writing on the danger of confusing the effects of grace with those of nature, she says: 'if the fact of staying outside the Church, on the threshold, gave me a feeling of superiority in relation to those who are inside, that would be a wrong position and perhaps I should have to enter. But for me it is bound up with a feeling of inferiority, which in the event is wholly advantageous.'[17] One might think that true humility lies in accepting the judgment of others, even favourable, in preference to one's own. It is obvious too that her relentless quest for absolute inferiority had progressed logically from the social and outward manifestations of her pre-conversion period to the spiritual realm, where it could more easily escape challenge, in her later years. Her conversion convinced her that her true Christian destiny was to remain deprived of the joys which those who stayed outside from ignorance or error would never know. If such an attitude cannot be reconciled, by definition, with the teachings of any church, it is surely compatible with Christ's call to follow him and be reviled by the world.

It can hardly be doubted that if she had lived, especially into the post-conciliar era, Simone Weil would have become a Catholic. It is enough in the context of this study to have shown that she was converted from an intensely idealistic form of humanism to be a follower of Christ, who alone fulfilled such humanism.

11

THOMAS MERTON

A man who writes a bestseller of more than four hundred pages on his conversion and subsequent monastic vocation, and who then spends half his final life-span (like Rancé; cosmic arithmetic can be strangely repetitive) to within a week or two in the same monastery, has at least a *prima facie* case for inclusion in these pages. As a Trappist he knew something, perhaps the wrong things, about Rancé, he found Simone Weil particularly interesting, and as a widely educated man he was almost certainly acquainted with the other stories already related, but he died just at the moment when the focus of his interest had shifted decisively from western to oriental spirituality. Thomas Merton can no more be categorized than the other converts, and only a dozen years after his death his figure cannot yet been seen in full perspective, but his very modernity helps to put some of the others in such perspective.

The events of his life are recounted with remarkable detail in his autobiography *The Seven Storey Mountain* (an abridged version goes under the title *Elected Silence*), extending from his birth in 1915 to April 1943, when he learned as a monk of his brother's death on active service. Thereafter his personal journals, and numerous other writings, take the story up to his death in 1968. The posthumous *Asian Journal*, edited and amplified by friends, and a comprehensive volume of intimate tributes, *Thomas Merton, Monk*, to which his former monastic superiors and other friends contributed with love and candour, are far from being the last word, but an assessment need not be delayed for lack of material. The problem is much more one of interpretation.

The great influence of his autobiography is a fact in itself, independent of the objective veracity of the book or the value accorded to particular opinions therein expressed. An English Benedictine, Aldhelm Cameron-Brown, very aptly calls it 'that swan-song of the nineteenth-century monastic revival'[1] and recalls that it was at one time forbidden reading for Benedictine novices (for fear that they might catch 'Cistercian fever'). The one clear fact about the book is that it genuinely represents what Merton thought, and wanted others to think, about his past life and his conversion at the time he wrote it in 1948. Some judgments are so superficial and patently absurd – Father Aldhelm rightly condemns Merton's account of Cambridge as simply ludicrous – as to cast serious doubt on others, but that is really beside the point: what influences his readers and what in retrospect influenced him is the causality established between such views and the conversion.

He was born at Prades, near the Pyrenees in France, in January 1915 of a New Zealand artist father and an American mother. Next year the family (later increased by another son) moved to America, where in 1921 his mother died of cancer. A very unsettled period followed, sometimes with his mother's parents in America, sometimes with his father in Bermuda and elsewhere, but in 1925 Thomas went to live in France, and until 1928 endured, and hated, the rigours of a *lycée* at Montauban. At least he learned French, and seems to have appreciated life in the tiny village where they lived. In 1928 his father took him to England, and from 1929–32 he was at Oakham, then a minor but not particularly nasty public school. There he was exposed to nothing much worse than English middle-class attitudes, Anglicanism, which he regarded as scarcely distinguishable, hardly religion at all, and a serious tooth infection.

In 1931 his father died of a brain tumour, and once the initial sadness had worn off Merton found himself 'completely stripped of everything that impeded the movement of my own will to do as it pleased: I imagined that I was free'.[2]

The context in which this freedom was exercised was first in London, where he stayed with his guardian, a doctor, and began to read such authors as D. H. Lawrence and Gide, and then, from 1933–34, in Cambridge, where he won a scholarship at Clare to read French and Italian. There is no reason to doubt that his adolescent emotions did in fact run riot at that time, or that he led a life of senseless dissipation, but it must also be said that the account of this period as given fifteen years later has about it a melodramatic ring fully justifying the word 'ludicrous' applied by Father Aldhelm, himself a more recent Cambridge product. How wicked he was, in what ways, at what cost to others and so on are questions that he does not attempt to resolve. Pride, selfishness and plain silliness seem to have been his basic sins. The shame and self-disgust were real enough at all events for him to abandon Cambridge and, as it turned out, Europe, for ever, in 1934. He returned to New York with relish and a mild dose of Communism.

Persuaded to continue a university education, he enrolled at Columbia in 1935, staying there until 1939, to take successively BA and MA. This, rather than the brief English phase, must be seen as that from which he was converted, but, again, the details of his worldly and aimless life are quite vague. He began to write, and became involved with student magazines; he found one or two teachers who fired him with their enthusiasm and set an example of integrity; he made numerous friends, mostly men, and so far as one can judge had no very serious (or at least satisfactory) relationships with girls. Intellectually he was wide-ranging but not very critical, and if his reflections of 1948 are reliable, he seems to have thought largely in stereotypes. 'Catholic', for example, was alien and sinister, 'Episcopalian', 'Protestant', 'Quaker' formal, arid and dull in varying degrees; Nazism was clearly evil, Communism no longer clearly good. Europe was decadent and corrupt, America materialistic and exciting, and war, in any case, could not be far away. In so far as he felt called to be or do anything, Merton wanted to be a writer, of novels and, perforce, of criticism for literary journals.

Between the beginning of 1937 and September 1938 a series of encounters with people and books began to move Merton in a particular direction. An interest in oriental mysticism began after he read Aldous Huxley's *Ends and Means*, though he characterized the mysticism there revealed as 'more or less useless'.[3] At about the same time he became quite friendly with a humble Indian monk, Bramachari, whose abbot had sent him from India to the World Fair at Chicago (where he arrived in fact too late to participate) and had stayed on in America. These first encounters with oriental spirituality do not seem to have been very decisive at the time, but in retrospect his later preoccupation with Asia clearly goes back to this source. More important was his discovery of Jacques Maritain's *Art and Scholasticism*, which he found directly relevant to the PhD thesis on William Blake on which he was then working. But more than any other single factor he reckoned that Etienne Gilson's *Spirit of Mediaeval Philosophy*, first read early in 1937, had set him on what subsequently proved his proper path.

As a result of these and similar influences a process lasting some eighteen months came to a recognizable conclusion.[4] 'By September 1938 the groundwork of conversion was more or less complete.' The proof that this was so came, for him, in the fact that he went to mass for the first time – leaving at the Sanctus which, as he later learned, marked the end of the so-called mass of the catechumens, when, in the early church and some missionary situations today, the unbaptized had to leave. He began to receive instruction from the young priest whose sermon on the incarnation had so impressed him at this first mass. In mid-November he was baptized: 'Because of the profound and complete conversion of my intellect, I thought I was entirely converted.'[5]

On the evidence of his own account, Merton had been transformed from a rootless agnostic, with a Protestant bias against everything Catholic, into an enthusiastic supporter of a neo-scholastic Catholicism who, moreover, practised the externals of religion with great fervour and frequency in a variety of New York churches. It is very clear that the 'Latin' element of his new-found faith particularly attracted him – his description of a visit to Cuba at Easter 1939 leaves no doubt on this score – and met an emotional, aesthetic and even social need as his previous Protestant experiences had never done. The presence of the poor and unlearned, the light and colour, as well as the mystery and antiquity, of the worship, the psychological release of the confessional, the spiritual power of the sacrament in eucharist or benediction, all these things and much else were integrated into an intellectually coherent system, through which all man's artistic, moral and material existence found meaning and justification. Merton had found his roots, and with them the strange freedom offered by total commitment; he had escaped from the prison of self. Or so he thought.

His hunger for full commitment expressed itself, predictably enough, in a prayer made solemnly (and privately) before the sacrament exposed at benediction, that God would make him a priest. Equally predictably, it was not long before he felt himself called to join a religious order. After quite thorough investigation and advice he picked on the Franciscans, the Friars Minor, and a date was duly appointed for him to enter the novitiate. It is really immaterial whether his choice was conditioned by romantic ideas about St Francis or by a serious call to a specific form of religious life; the crisis that struck him might equally well have occurred in the context of that or any other choice. As he relates it, he was reading the Book of Job one day when out of the blue he was struck by an overwhelming sense of his own past sins and present unworthiness. He realized, though it seems most odd, that none of those with whom he had discussed his vocation knew about the foul (but unspecified) iniquities of his past; that God, through the authorities, would surely cast him out once the truth was known; that, in a word, he was not fit to offer himself for the religious life. So he withdrew his application, in great distress, and set about the task of reorientating himself.

His own comments on what had happened, written down nine years or so after the event, are informative about himself, and deserve at least to be considered in the similar case of others.[6] 'The false humility of hell is an unending, burning shame at the inescapable stigma of our sins. . . It is only when we have lost all love of our selves for our own sakes that our past sins cease to give us any cause for suffering or for the anguish of shame. For the saints, when they remember their sins, do not remember the sins but the mercy of God. . . ' Such wise words are the mature product of the conversion, the state they describe is the counter-part to the first unthinking enthusiasm of the neophyte.

By now war had broken out, and Merton did not know when, or even whether, he would be drafted. While he tried to sort things out he took a teaching post at St Bonaventura's, a Francis-can college of university status in up-state New York. He lived as closely as possible the life of a religious, saying canonical hours, for example, in the intervals of trying to teach English literature to young men of minimal academic attainment. His first medical examination found him unfit for service (because so many of his teeth were missing) and a week or two later he went to spend Easter 1941 at Gethsemani. He had first heard of this huge Trapp-ist monastery in Kentucky a year before, but did not really know very much about the Cistercian life until he started reading about it in preparation for his visit. As he describes it eight years later, 'the embers . . . had broken into flame . . . within me',[7] and he suddenly again felt the mysterious pull of the cloister. This time he did not allow himself to be carried away by premature convic-tion, and made the long journey to Kentucky in a cautious frame of mind.

His first, and lasting, impressions of Gethsemani were deeply moving, but he was afraid to face openly the question of a vocation which the 'false humility' had apparently closed a year before. In his own words, Holy Week was 'a mute, hopeless, interior strug-gle'.[8] But before he finished his retreat he prayed that he might have the grace of a Trappist vocation.

On his return to St Bonaventura's he was tormented by what he himself calls the 'dream' of his vocation, fearing the reality which would either finally expose his inadequacy or force him to take the responsibility of accepting Cistercian life. He is candid enough to mention his 'other dream' of becoming a Carthusian. At that time there were no houses of that ultimately austere order in America, and there could be no question of joining one in war-torn Europe, but it is typical of the fantasy world in which Merton still partly lived that he cherished this impossible idea purely as a dream.

The last few months before his final decision show both the uncertainty, perhaps restlessness would be a better word, of his nature and the quite specific call to a particular place. During the summer he became involved in a project directed by a White Russian, Baroness de Hueck, for bringing some kind of hope and feeling of human dignity to the Negro slum-dwellers of Harlem. For at least a week or two Merton wondered whether this noble work might not be his true vocation. The deep-seated social conscience which had made him react against certain aspects of English middle-class life and flirt with Communism in fact never left him in peace, but it seems most unlikely that he would have been successful, let alone happy, working for any length of time in Harlem. After Harlem he went for a retreat to a Cistercian house on Rhode Island, much nearer than Gethsemani to New York. As he says, the Cistercian life led there earned his complete respect, but he felt no special desire to enter that particular monastery. By his own account the next significant step was his discovery, in October, of St Thérèse of Lisieux, in his view the greatest saint of the past three hundred years. Meditation on St Thérèse, further meetings with Baroness de Hueck, fervent prayer, finally advice and support from one of the friars, all helped to bring about the final decision.

In early December he wrote to ask the abbot of Gethsemani if he might come and spend Christmas there, and was just rejoicing in the abbot's welcoming reply, when he had another summons to attend a medical examination. This he answered with a plea for deferment on the grounds that he was about to test his monastic vocation. A few days later America entered the war. He was granted one month's deferment and on 10 December 1941 returned to Gethsemani, this time as a postulant. Twenty-seven years later to the day he died, still a monk of Gethsemani, still searching.

From baptism to Gethsemani had taken three years, and in one

sense that may be reckoned the period of his conversion. In the
light of what happened, however, and was still happening up to
the very moment of his death, the next twenty-seven years show
unmistakably that conflict and uncertainty were far from resolved
in 1941; indeed, in some vital respects, were intensified. From the
start of his monastic experience two factors threatened the stability
which should thenceforth have characterized his life. He found
many traditional aspects of the Reformed Cistercian rule pointless
and unattractive, criticizing, for example, what he called 'the
unseasoned jargon of transliterated French'[9] in which American
religious had to seek their spiritual nourishment. Monastic obedience is not the same as uncritical acquiescence, but the tone of
Merton's criticism could hardly be echoed by more than a few
within a given community without provoking serious problems of
discipline. The other factor is partly connected with this; Merton
always felt himself to be a writer, and his superiors actively
encouraged him to write. Thus his reflections on monastic life and
much else were widely disseminated and had considerable influence inside and outside the cloister, even if they never became
normative. Perhaps more serious for Merton himself was the problem of identity inevitably posed by this dual mode of existence.

He himself put it in very strong terms in the Epilogue to his
autobiography. By 1944, when he took simple vows, he should
have resolved the problem of identity one way or another, 'but,'
he writes, 'there was this shadow, this double, this writer who had
followed me into the cloister . . . I cannot lose him. He still wears
the name of Thomas Merton. Is it the name of an enemy? He is
supposed to be dead. Nobody seems to understand that one of us
has got to die.'[10] Even the duality of nomenclature is significant;
in the monastery, and in all ecclesiastical contexts, he lived as
Father Louis, affectionately known as 'Louie', but he wrote as
Thomas Merton, and by virtually all his outside friends and corres-
pondents was never known as anything else. In his last days he
apologized to an audience in Calcutta for appearing before them
'in disguise', in a clerical collar, rather than in his usual costume
of blue jeans and sports shirt. When in the same period he paid
a visit to the Dalai Lama he was prevailed upon, rightly, as he
admits, to wear (and be photographed in) his Cistercian habit:
'yet recognizing that it is at odds with my own policy of *not*
appearing as a monk, a priest, a cleric "in the world" '.[11] In the
same order of things the *Asian Journal* frequently comments on
the standard of food in the restaurants he visited, the beer, rum
or other drinks he ordered while travelling and so on. Whether or

not these details are important in themselves, they undeniably reveal a man who had no time for the letter of the law – and who was busy up to the moment of his death attempting to define the spirit of that law in terms acceptable to himself.

What seems clear is that from the time he entered Gethsemani until he died his conversion continued to work upon him, producing often painful tensions which remained unresolved. His previous aimless, or vaguely self-centred, existence had been replaced by a life dedicated to the service of God, and from that there could be no going back, but the precise nature of his vocation was as obscure as the call was imperative. In 1949 he was ordained priest, thus completing in a sense the course of instruction inaugurated by his decision to seek baptism in 1938, and from 1951–55 as Master of Students, then from 1955–65 as Master of Novices, he was occupied in passing on that instruction to others. Such responsible posts, second in influence perhaps only to that of abbot, held for so considerable a period, prove beyond question Merton's ability and willingness to lead the traditional monastic life of a Cistercian. His success in these tasks is partly reflected in the proposal, which he refused with firm civility, to elect him abbot, first of another, later of his own, monastery. It is hard to believe that he would have proved suitable.

In a strictly factual record of his monastic life his next step, after laying down the Mastership of Novices, suggests a deeper, more intense spiritual life. In his last three years he secured permission, reluctantly granted in stages, to withdraw to a hermitage (a simple but adequate cabin) in the vast grounds of the monastery, some fifteen minutes' walk away, and was assigned a monk as secretary to help him deal with his voluminous correspondence. This quest for still greater solitude became almost obsessive, and coupled with a desire to escape. In the last weeks of his life his journal records: 'The lack of quiet and general turbulence there [in the hermitage], external and internal, are indications that I ought to move. And so far the indications seem to point to Alaska or to the area round the Redwoods [California].'[12] A little earlier he had written: 'for solitude, Alaska really seems to be the very best place.'[13] But the usual associations of the word 'solitude' are certainly at odds with what he goes on to say: 'The idea of being in Alaska and then going out to Japan or the US strikes me as a rather good solution . . . On the way back from this trip I think I will need to go to Europe [Scotland, Wales and Switzerland to talk about oriental spirituality and visit communities living in oriental style],' and: 'I have needed the experience of this journey. Much as the hermitage has meant, I have been needing to get away from Gethsemani and it was long over-due.' The repetition of 'need' and the quite explicit restlessness (in a man of fifty-three) are above all remarkable for the fact that, unlike the great majority of monks, even of ordinary men with the usual domestic and economic constraints of that age, he was granted, and seemed to expect, the freedom and material means to indulge it.

There is another aspect to the same thing which has already been mentioned in connection with Merton's identity crisis. In 1944 he wrote of his fear of that double, Thomas Merton the writer, but he had not by then had any chance to see where this *alter ego* (but for the fact that he died in Bangkok, 'Siamese twin' might be a better description) would lead him. His superiors used their discretion in encouraging him to go on writing, and when his fame brought him closer contacts with the outside world than most Trappists ever know or want, it is hardly surprising that, as a man of conscience, he got drawn into such major issues as civil rights and the Vietnam war. The mere title of one of his books, *Conjectures of a Guilty Bystander*, is self-explanatory. It is not necessary to equate the contemplative life with escapism in order to feel misgivings about the wisdom of such public involvement on the part of a man vowed to silence and solitude; it was he, after all, who chose, indeed asked, to join the Cistercian Order at Gethsemani. In a vital sense Merton's conversion did not cause him to 'leave the world'. On a more private level it did not cause him either to restrict his contacts by letter or even meeting with men and women who were drawn to him as a person and a writer just as they would have been if he had never become a monk of an enclosed order. His spontaneous response to freedom, on his first journey abroad for nearly thirty years, is vividly recounted in his *Asian Journal*. The world of airport bars, luxury hotels, diplomatic parties and so on is one to which he adapts with ease, just as he reacts with wonder and curiosity to the Asian scene, including its spiritual manifestations.

Obviously Merton was a man who thrived on tension, inner and outer, and it would be absurd and pedantic to judge his monastic or spiritual life in purely literal terms. Nevertheless, things said by him and about him so consistently reveal an instability, perhaps one should say insecurity, at the heart of his personality as to prompt doubts about the totality of his conversion. A fellow monk, later elected abbot of another monastery,[14] emphasizes Merton's deep natural tendency to inconsistency and even self-contradiction in speech and writing, and links this with Merton's feeling that he had no real home (which did not prevent him asserting frequently that Gethsemani was home to him). Some of the examples given are quite trivial – enthusiastic superlatives about some poet who would be dismissed a day or two later as dull – but are perhaps all the more revealing. As for Merton's own position, one or two phrases sufficiently illustrate the inherent dichotomy. He writes in *Contemplation in a World of Action*: 'Fidelity to tedious but predictable rule can become an easy substitute for fidelity, in openness and risk, to the unpredictable word,'[15] but one is tempted to add that infidelity to such a rule is not a good in itself. In the chapter on 'Vocation' in *No Man Is an Island* come two strangely self-revealing observations: 'Some people find, in the end, that they have made many wrong guesses and that their paradoxical vocation is to go through life guessing wrong. It takes them a long time to find out that they are happier that way', and, 'the one thing that really decides a vocation is the *ability to make a firm decision* to embrace a certain state and *to act on that decision.*'[16] That was written in 1955; thirteen years later the Asian journey and the embryonic decision to settle in Alaska or California suggests that he was still making wrong guesses, but that he had a multiple, or evolving, vocation.

If death had not prevented him, he would quite certainly have gone still deeper into the oriental, especially Zen, mysticism which had begun to preoccupy him more and more from about 1960. A meeting with the Zen master, Suzuki, in 1961 (for which he had special permission to travel to New York) led him ever further into study of this spirituality, culminating in *Zen and the Birds of Appetite* published in the year of his death. He was particularly attracted by the freedom, 'limitlessness . . . lack of inhibition . . . psychic fullness of creativity'[17] which, in his view, Zen shared with gospel Christianity. A week or two before he died he reacted thus to the advice that he should seek a Tibetan guru: 'Why not? The question is finding the right man. I am not exactly dizzy with the idea of looking for a magic master, but I would certainly like to learn something by experience.'[18]

Like Simone Weil, but unlike Charles de Foucauld, Thomas Merton was impelled by conversion to start on a journey, physical and spiritual, which never brought him to a place of rest. The long years, half a lifetime, at Gethsemani demonstrated beyond doubt that Merton's call to serve God in that place was genuine, if not necessarily final. Those who had to suffer from his volatile nature, his often pungent criticism, his intransigent independence

– and none suffered more than his successive abbots – are quick
to acknowledge his goodness, his sincerity, his ultimate obedience.
In all those years he left the monastery only three times, including
medical visits, and it is a most extraordinary irony that his first
extended journey should have been his last.

Invited to a congress of Asian Catholic religious in Bangkok,
on the strength of his reputation and interest in oriental spirituality, Merton had planned a comprehensive tour of exploration.
He had already been to Ceylon, Madras, Calcutta, Darjeeling and
Thailand when he was killed by a faulty electric fan in his hotel
at Bangkok. He planned to go to Indonesia, Hong Kong and
Japan before making his way back via Europe. It is pointless to
ask what would have become of him if he had lived – he had no
idea himself – but it is more than symbolically fitting that his body
was flown back in one of those US Air Force planes whose presence in the Far East he had campaigned against, to be buried in
the cemetery at Gethsemani. Only in death did he find stability
and, one hopes, rest.

Conclusions

Apart from St Paul, whose biography will always remain too sketchy to permit of any firm conclusions, twelve very varied characters have been considered in the preceding chapters in as much detail as possible. They range over some sixteen centuries of Christianity, and it is clear that a mere dozen individuals, however different, cannot sum up so vast a period, but within the criteria discussed at the beginning these twelve men and women cover a sufficiently wide range of conversion experience to invite certain conclusions.

Statistically the most conspicuous imbalance in the list is between men and women, and between Catholics and Protestants, but the list is not meant to be statistically significant. The two women chosen happen both to be Jewish, both of this century, but quite different in the paths they respectively took after conversion. The three Protestants, Luther, Bunyan and Booth, belong to three different centuries and three very different traditions. Luther's conversion took him out of the Catholic church, Merton's took him from nominal Anglicanism into the Catholic church. There is no question of proportional representation in the selection of these twelve; they are individuals, not types, above all not stereotypes. Those who share the same, or similar, historical background, like Luther and Loyola, Pascal and Rancé, Simone Weil and Edith Stein, may differ as much from each other as those who do not.

With regard to women, their social status until recent times so limited the range of options open to them that the great majority of women converts through the centuries would be adequately represented by two or three cases of penitent sinners, expiating their usually sexual delinquency in a convent, like Louise de la Vallière, Louis XIV's mistress, or in virtually monastic seclusion but without vows, like Madame de Longueville, Louis' cousin, or of Protestant ladies, like the wife of George Fox, the Quaker, or Serena, Countess of Huntingdon, the Methodist, giving themselves up to piety and good works. It can hardly be doubted that as many women as men have known conversion experiences, but with rare exceptions the accounts are less interesting and the influence more restricted. As with women, so with Jews; it was only when emancipation freed them from overwhelming social disabilities that a genuinely free choice of response to conversion became possible. Most Catholic books on conversion quote the early example of the brothers Théodore and Alphonse Ratisbonne, born Jews in Alsace early in the nineteenth century, both converted to Catholicism, and the latter founder of a religious order (of Notre-Dame de Sion) for working with Jews (1842). It would not be difficult to multiply examples of such highly interesting Jewish, or female, converts, though perhaps few of the names would be very well known, but it is questionable whether further examples from under-represented categories would substantially alter the conclusions to be drawn from these dozen cases.

Except for Simone Weil (thirty-four) and Pascal (thirty-nine), and possibly Francis (forty-five), none can be said to have died young, though Edith Stein and Foucauld were both murdered and Merton died in an accident. Nine or ten of these dozen lives therefore measure an average span. It may be pure coincidence, but only Pascal and Simone Weil were not in orders, either as religious or priests or the equivalent. The three Protestants were all married and, again perhaps pure coincidence, the only ones who could be described as being of modest background. Luther's father had come up in the world, Booth's had gone down, as Bunyan's probably had, and it is misleading to call them working-class, but in comparison with the patrician Augustine, Loyola, Rancé, Foucauld and the comfortably bourgeois Francis, Pascal, Edith Stein and Simone Weil, the Protestants are undeniably social inferiors. Educationally the qualifications are rather oddly distributed: the privileged Francis and Loyola, the indigent Bunyan and Booth received somewhat sketchy early education for very different reasons, though Loyola and Booth went on to study, while all the others were intellectually outstanding, even Foucauld, who followed fairly undistinguished early studies with work of abiding value in geography and linguistics.

The nationalities of the twelve show the same wide variety: Pascal, Rancé and Foucauld were all French; Simone Weil born French of partly German Jewish stock; Bunyan was English, Booth English with some Jewish blood; Merton born in France of a New Zealand father and American mother; Edith Stein born German of partly East European Jewish stock; Luther German,

Loyola Basque, Francis Italian with perhaps some French connection; Augustine a Roman African. No one ethnic or cultural
element predominates, but all lived in societies where nominal
Christians formed the majority of the population.

From all these considerations it should follow that a pattern, or
patterns, common to the wide variety of persons composing this
selected dozen should illustrate something of general relevance to
Christian conversion as such.

It is a commonplace that conversion, of whatever kind, follows
a period of emotional confusion and disturbance, often, but not
always, accompanied by intellectual doubts. A feature of the
twelve lives under analysis is the marked tension or imbalance in
family relationships. All before the age of sixteen, and in five
cases before they were six, Loyola, Pascal, Rancé, Bunyan, Foucauld and Merton had lost their mother, and Booth, Edith Stein
and Foucauld again their father. Of the remainder, Augustine was
nineteen when he lost his father, and his close relations with his
mother remained extremely tense until he was baptized only a
year before she died; Luther incurred his father's fury by becoming a friar when he was twenty-two, and was probably not fully
reconciled until he broke with Rome; Francis' relations with his
father were always uneasy, and total estrangement from both
parents followed his conversion; Simone Weil was on good terms
with her parents and her brother, but they apparently knew
nothing of her spiritual evolution until some time after her death.
One cannot usefully speak of norms either physically, because we
know too little of expectation of life at the widely differing periods
involved, or emotionally, because parent-child relationships also
vary so widely in different classes and cultures, but it is obviously
significant that five out of the dozen knew only one parent from
infancy, and of those who knew both strong tensions are recorded
in every case except that of Simone Weil.

In the same affective context, what is known of extra-familial
relationships is also significant. Augustine contracted his liaison
and became a father at about the same time as his conversion to
Manichaeism first estranged him from his mother, and he had put
away his concubine, and in effect his Manichaeism, shortly before
his conversion to Christianity. Francis and Loyola may well have
been frivolous, but the evidence does not suggest that they were
any more sexually experienced than the very austere Luther,
whose marriage came too long after his conversion to affect it.
Pascal and Rancé had women friends, and Rancé may have been
infatuated with Mme de Montbazon, but they both almost cer-

tainly stopped short of physical involvement and formed no lasting relationship. The same is true for the relations of Edith Stein and Simone Weil with men. Foucauld certainly, Merton very probably, had affairs with women of varying intensity and short duration, and were to that extent sexually experienced. Bunyan buried his first wife and remarried, Booth had more than twenty years of widowhood; both of them, like Luther, were happily married and had several children.

The difference between the three Protestants and all the others is notable; not one of the other nine felt able to combine the conversion experience with family life, though all, except the priest Rancé, were perfectly free to do so. Bunyan and Booth saw their wives and families as part of the whole service to which they were called, and inevitable victims of any persecution or privation they might incur, but also, without doubt, the immediate source and object of the human affection they needed to receive and bestow. One cannot be sure what Pascal and Simone Weil would have chosen had they lived longer, but the seven others all joined, or created, a religious community (even if Foucauld's projected order was only fully realized after his death) which provided emotional stability and fellowship. The only one of the twelve whose life was not markedly austere after conversion was Luther, who in fact abandoned austerity in the second part of his life. Most of the others can properly be called puritans, particularly the married Bunyan and Booth. It is an odd illusion of celibates that marriage and asceticism are incompatible, and the choice of marriage rather than celibacy had nothing to do with pleasure and self-indulgence, except perhaps in Luther's case, though the need for a supportive relationship in a cruelly exposed ministry clearly has. All, without exception, were warm and faithful friends, giving and receiving affection generously. The persistent popular belief that a religious life is the natural refuge for spinsters of both sexes, or for jilted lovers, is not borne out in these twelve, who are not so much emotionally inadequate as strongly oriented in a different direction.

A sense of isolation, of loneliness even in the midst of friends, seems to have been the common experience of all these people, but there is a further characteristic which seems more specific. Merton and Edith Stein alone of the twelve followed their conversion by putting themselves formally under obedience for life in a religious community, and while Merton was a loyal monk to successive abbots, his interpretation of monastic obedience was idiosyncratic, to say the least. Luther, Loyola, Rancé and Booth were very autocratic, so was Augustine in a slightly different way. Francis was for a long time an uncompromising leader of his order until overwhelmed by opposition, and Foucauld was so uncompromising that his order never materialized in his lifetime. Bunyan could have come out of gaol at any time by submitting to the civil authority, Simone Weil spent most of her short life rebelling against authority of all kinds. Pascal obeyed no one, except his director in certain things, and never sacrificed his independence to anyone. Even Edith Stein never accepted her director's objections to her Carmelite vocation, and submitted willingly to obedience only when she had at last taken the veil, even then finding many details of the life irksome. In their different ways all were quite exceptionally independent individuals, unlike so many converts (so many indeed of those they themselves converted) who ask nothing better than to spend the rest of their lives under the rules and directions imposed from above. Such passive humility is far more common than the active humility of those whose lifelong struggle is against their own pride.

When it comes to analysing the actual conversion experience, a formal difficulty arises in many of the cases from the nature and timing of the record. Augustine waited ten years to write the *Confessions*, Loyola reluctantly dictated his autobiography more than thirty years after the event, Merton waited ten years, Bunyan between ten and twenty (the date is uncertain), and the others divulged scraps of information, written or oral, over periods ranging from three years for Simone Weil to thirty or more for Luther and Booth. Pascal is the only one to record the experience when it happened, and but for the miraculous survival of that bit of parchment no one would ever have known. Rancé charted the course of his conversion in a series of contemporary letters, and of course unrecorded conversations, but these describe the effect and not the nature of the experience, which he cryptically alluded to only thirty years later. Even Paul's conversion has to be judged from documents written twenty years later.

This delay in no way impugns the veracity of the various accounts, and indeed in most cases is a guarantee that the experience marks a total and lasting change of heart, but it does inevitably mean reading history backwards. In some cases the literary form chosen is demonstrably not compatible with an objective, literal statement of events. The filiation of some accounts with identifiable models adds a further factor to complicate interpretation. Augustine's '*tolle, lege*' must be taken as a literary, not a literal, statement. Luther was deeply influenced by Paul at the time of his own crisis, and had also read Augustine closely, and may well have simplified and dramatized the *Turmerlebnis* when he much later came to talk and write about it. Bunyan refers explicitly to the influence on him of Luther's *Commentary on Galatians*. Pascal and Rancé were familiar with both Paul and Augustine. Booth certainly knew Paul, and later Luther, as well as the ample Wesleyan conversion literature. Foucauld is known to have been reading Bossuet, another Augustinian. Loyola had been struck by the story of Francis, Edith Stein by that of Teresa of Avila. Of course, most of these people had read other books which had not impressed them in the same way, and the process of selection must have continued long after the conversion experience so that one writer rather than another became specially associated with it.

Partly because of the formal pattern established, especially in Protestant conversion literature, partly because of the difficulty in describing to others any intimate and powerful experience, one should be wary of interpreting too literally converts' reports of voices and visions. That some message, probably verbal, or insight was given to them need not be questioned; that it took the form of, for instance, the blinding light or the heavenly voice of the road to Damascus is possible, but not certain. Even in modern examples, such assertions can never be authenticated as can such physical phenomena as the stigmata. What can be authenticated of the inner experience is the spiritual aura, the charisma in current jargon, of the person who has received it, either through their presence or their writings. They know they are no longer what they were, and normally refer to their former state as one of sin; they have seen enough of what they are seeking to recognize it and show it forth to others.

As has already been observed, conversion follows a period of emotional disturbance, and of its nature involves a break with the past to which the emotions refer. In the Puritan schema the first stage was called 'conviction of sin', and was followed by 'vocation or calling', the feeling that an unmerited love marked the sinner out for salvation. This in turn was followed by 'justification', achievement of a saving faith, and 'sanctification', the growth of holiness of life, to which 'glorification' was the ultimate end. It is interesting to see how this schema (excellently presented in Sharrock's introduction to *Grace Abounding*) corresponds with the conversion experiences of others besides Bunyan. Luther and Booth, as one might expect, Pascal and Rancé, following their master Augustine, but also Loyola, Foucauld and Merton can be seen to have gone through these stages. The emphasis on sin (in the sense of evildoing) is replaced in Edith Stein's account by the acceptance of Christ's love and what looks like recognition of sins of omission, and Simone Weil's formula 'gravity and grace' refers to a similar concept. Francis specifically associated his encounter with the leper with ending his time of sin (and by implication inaugurating a time of love), but we do not know what exact inner experience prompted him to make that particular gesture. Bunyan's faith, and the schema just quoted, was Calvinist, and must be seen in the context of predestination, so that it is all the more remarkable that Booth, who abhorred that doctrine, as well as all the Catholics should exhibit so similar a pattern.

The sin of which these people are convinced varies greatly and is in some cases complicated by intellectual doubts. For Augustine and Pascal, intellectual pride had set up the main obstacle to saving grace; for Edith Stein and Simone Weil, looking at Christianity from the outside, the need for intellectual conviction was probably secondary by the time of their conversion to their emotional needs; and this is also probably true of Merton. A generally aimless and self-indulgent life seems to lie behind the conversion of Francis, Loyola, Rancé, Foucauld and again Merton, while Luther, Bunyan and Booth were moved by more profound misgivings about the state of their souls rather than specific misdeeds (except perhaps for Booth's pencil-case). All except Augustine explicitly link their conversion experience with a realization of Christ's saving love for them, and Augustine's silence on that score by no means proves that he felt differently from the others. Pascal, Rancé and the three Protestants took hell and the power of evil very seriously, and the ex-Manichaean Augustine added to his spiritual awareness long familiarity with the intellectual concept of evil. The others were probably less moved by fear of eternal retribution than by thirst for a love they could not find in earthly things. All in their different ways were unusually self willed individuals who quite suddenly revolted against the insatiable demands of self and submitted to God's love revealed in Christ's suffering. In one way or another self-love, usually in the form of pride, was the sin of which they all became aware. Those who felt justified in the technical theological sense and those who in a more general sense felt a surge of new strength and purpose were clearly at one in ascribing their grace to Christ and his redemptive work.

After the shock of the initial experience, the next step is crucial; like the seed falling among thorns or on stony ground, conversion can be short-lived or abortive. Two points at once emerge: all those converted to Catholicism (or within the Catholic church already) automatically enter upon the sacramental discipline of that church. The sacraments as means of grace are equally available to all Catholics, but converts additionally gain from the sacrament of penance a confessor whose regular advice they must heed, and who may become spiritual director (that is, an adviser outside the context of penance) unless, or until, there is someone else. Preparation for baptism (Augustine, Edith Stein), for reception into the church (Merton) or general confession (Loyola, Pascal, Foucauld) are different ways in which the individual comes under the influence of a particular priest. Even Simone Weil, who fought shy of baptism, accepted direction from Perrin. Of the Protestants, Luther continued his normal priestly practice and even said his daily office (sometimes accumulated for days) until he was finally excommunicated, after which he admitted no spiritual superior and two sacraments only, baptism and communion, which he conscientiously administered. Bunyan was received into the Bedford church by total immersion baptism and looked up to Mr Gifford as pastor; Booth followed the Wesleyan practice of sacraments (he did not need to be re-baptized after his Anglican christening) and bowed to the authority of local ministers without, apparently, turning to any one person for guidance. In a word, all joined, or joined more fervently, in the discipline and practice of their church (and Simone Weil went to mass, even though she could not take communion), except Luther, who set up what amounted to his own church, which he claimed to be the only true one.

The second point is inseparable from the first: the conversion experience in all these cases was an entirely private affair. Whatever influence each of the twelve underwent, they were no more converted by another person than Paul had been. When Foucauld knelt down at Huvelin's bidding, made his confession and then his communion, he had for some time been under the influence both of Huvelin and Marie Bondy, but the moment of conversion, the decision to seek out Huvelin in church and talk to him, was personal and independent. At most Huvelin was the catalyst. All through his life Augustine had been exposed to his mother's Christian influence, and he was unquestionably right to emphasize her part in his conversion, but the actual experience was independent of her and set off by a quite different set of reflections. The same could be shown of each of the twelve converts.

The point is important, and clearly helps to distinguish what may usefully be called a primary from a secondary conversion experience. Not one of the twelve could feel that conversion had been imposed either by circumstances or the dominating influence of another person. The defeat, and surrender, of their pride and self-will was the outcome of a direct transaction between each of them and God. They in their turn converted incalculable, but in most cases large, numbers of people, either by their preaching and example, from Augustine and Francis to Booth and Foucauld; or by their writings and example, from Pascal to Merton; and it is these latter converts who belong to the tradition inaugurated in scripture by Philip and the Ethiopian eunuch. With the possible exception of Luther (and he constantly sought advice from Staupitz and others) it is an effect, not a cause of the conversion experience that these primary converts seek guidance and support from others. It is noteworthy that throughout the ages those who have claimed some special and direct illumination and have thereafter not submitted themselves to the counsel of others or the discipline of a church (like so many of the sectarian leaders of the sixteenth and seventeenth centuries) have been more conspicuous for the short-term enthusiasm they inspired than for any lasting movement.

If the stage immediately following the conversion experience involves a visible act and change of life, the 'vocation' and 'sanctification' stages are much less clear and definite than, for example, the act of baptism. The initial experience closes the way back to the past, but in none of the twelve cases does it lead directly to the long-term future. Spiritual anguish of an acute kind, Luther's *Anfechtungen* or Bunyan's 'temptations to despair', Loyola's trials at Manresa, Rancé's arduous journey towards the one solution at which his every instinct rebelled, Booth's long struggles with frustrating patterns of ministry, Foucauld's abortive Trappist experiment, Edith Stein's frustration at being denied entry to Carmel, Merton's last minute panic and abandonment of a Franciscan vocation, all these and similar experiences were testing in a fruitful and positive way, and to that extent different from the confusion and emptiness preceding conversion. None the less, the imperative call heard, however, indistinctly, at that first moment did not in these cases give way to unclouded serenity or certainty, as it undoubtedly did to many of their own later disciples. The strident assertion of self-will and pride is not to be stilled in an instant, and the decision to replace love of self by love of God, even aided by the sacraments and wise spiritual mentors, may take long and painful effort to implement.

Theologically the Puritan schema quoted above is no doubt applicable to most conversions, but in practice it refers to a set of options socially, religiously, even physically too limited to do justice to the choices confronting even the Protestants among the twelve. To take a specific example, Foucauld felt an absolute need after his conversion to take the humblest place; he felt an overwhelming attraction for the Holy Land and in particular for Nazareth, where Christ had spent the hidden years which had such deep spiritual significance for Foucauld. Once he had left the Trappists and established himself with the Franciscan sisters at Nazareth and then Jerusalem, it was not temptation or the struggle against sin that made him restless, but the inner nagging belief that he was called to some other form of sanctification, as yet unrevealed. His initially reluctant acceptance of ordination, his return to the Sahara, his obviously valuable ministry with soldiers and native Algerians, brought him ever nearer his goal, but it was only when he at last settled down with the Touaregs, twenty years after his conversion, that he knew he was where he was meant to be.

It took Booth nearly as long to make his way from the apostolate in the Nottingham slums to his Christian Mission at Mile End and the Salvation Army, and Loyola spent thirteen years between Manresa and those first Jesuit vows taken on Montmartre. Definitions are not equally precise in all cases, and the early deaths of Pascal and Simone Weil make any judgment of what their lives might have been if spared hazardous if not pointless, but in all the other cases conversion, and even sanctification, did not lead easily or automatically to the final phase.

The roots of self-love go deeper than most of us might care to acknowledge, and men and women as individualistic as these twelve do not easily eradicate self-will. It is therefore all the more remarkable that when that harsh, and often prolonged, struggle had been won, the succeeding stages of conversion should have shown even more clearly their extreme individualism brought to the service of God and others. A striking feature of all these twelve is the absolute specificity of their vocation. Even reading history backwards, there is no predictable or inevitable causal chain leading Francis to the stigmata or Edith Stein to Auschwitz. In the latter case, indeed, Carmel should, and could, have meant safety. The defective fan in Bangkok interrupted Merton's plans for entering upon a new form of monastic life, to embrace oriental and other traditions. Terminal illness robbed the world of Pascal's *Apology* and left instead the fragmentary *Pensées*, arguably more influential than any finished product would have been. On a strictly pragmatic basis each one of the twelve counts for what he or she was, not might have been.

Conversion is often described as a rebirth, an entering upon a new life with the past erased, but such a definition is in many ways misleading. Repentance, *metanoia*, conversion, implies total change, but of priorities, not of the components of life and personality. All conversions are not lived out to the end, backsliding in an ever present danger, so it is not surprising that extremes of mortification, spiritual even more than physical, are a regular feature of the convert's new life. The old life is at first rejected root and branch – the deliberate physical squalor Francis and Loyola imposed on themselves is an extreme example – but is subsequently reintegrated into a new framework. Pascal did not renounce mathematics, Foucauld became a still more distinguished Arabist and linguist, Edith Stein approached Carmelite mysticism with the unwanted perspective of a phenomenologist, but these gifts and talents were transformed after conversion by being subordinated to a higher purpose. Self-love had been destroyed, or brought under control, but the self, the essential personality, far from being destroyed found ever fuller expression. Francis' identification with Christ's humanity hastened his physical death but brought him spiritual perfection.

The sheer energy of these twelve after conversion is amazing. Many of them, like Pascal or Simone Weil, suffered from real ill-health, but they all performed prodigious feats of endurance. Francis, Loyola, Foucauld, Booth covered quite extraordinary distances, often on foot; Luther, Merton, Bunyan, even the cloistered Rancé, preached or wrote astounding numbers of letters, tracts, sermons and the like; Pascal composed one of the world's masterpieces when mortally sick. Their energy was superhuman, and may legitimately be recognized as supernatural. It is not easy for people of such demonic energy to harness it completely, and many of them were imprudent and impetuous, but when we see what they achieved after conversion it is easier to appreciate what such energy applied to selfish ends would have effected. They kept nothing back, and most of them alarmed their friends with their almost wanton disregard of health and safety.

Implicit in the initial experience of conversion was absolute, unconditional acceptance of demands, as yet obscure and unformed, which would not cease until death. Conversion for these twelve meant total commitment, a leap in the dark, sustained by faith. It meant, too, in every case an acceptance of

God's love, revealed in Christ, that is to say, not an abstract ideal or a material programme, but a living relationship, vulnerable like all relationships to doubt, fear or betrayal on our part. Readiness to accept failure, real or apparent, is part of commitment. By ordinary human standards, let alone the standards they set themselves, many of these twelve died having failed to do what they set out to do; Francis at odds with his order, Rancé forced to see his abbey rent by dissension, Booth defied by some of his children, Foucauld without one recruit to his long-planned order, these and almost all the others died disappointed by those they had tried to inspire, but never for one moment doubting God's love for them or betraying their trust. There is no way in which we can verify 'glorification', though presumptive evidence may be very strong, but the survival of the spirit of these men and women in their different works, whether in disciples or written work, often after a period of obscurity, error or dispute, is one indication at human level of divine favour. In the case of those identified with institutions (Francis, Loyola, Rancé, Booth, Foucauld) which their successors have often changed greatly, not always for the better, it is probably more important that they have the ability to recreate for the reader discovering their actual life and teaching for the first time something of the power transmitted to and through them in their lifetime.

The dreadful crimes committed through the ages, down to our own day, in the name of Christ, wilfully and all too often sincerely, should warn us against judging individuals by their alleged followers. It is even less satisfactory to judge conversion experiences by canons of orthodoxy laid down by particular religious authorities. There must be a relationship between one's view of the church and one's view of the truth, but personal preference or even deep conviction regarding the nature of the church should not lead to rigid definitions of what is right or wrong, good or bad, in conversion. The experiences discussed in this book, and the lives to which they gave rise, represent a private transaction between God and the convert. That transaction is in every case validated and communicated to others, if at all, by faith in Christ's saving grace, offered to all as the conversion experience cannot be. Just like Paul, these twelve men and women have no other credentials as Christians than what they saw of Christ and showed to others. Paul alone saw the risen Christ as those who had walked with the Lord had done; all others since have seen his presence and his truth in some different way. It is not their piety or their kindness, their learning or their eloquence that mark them out but the manner of their calling.

It is significant that Loyola is the last of the Catholic converts studied to have been canonized. The cause for Foucauld's beatification is active, and may eventually prove successful, but Pascal and Rancé, both in their own day regarded by many as potential saints of the church, Edith Stein and Thomas Merton seem most unlikely to receive such recognition. Nor, in a less formal sense, are the claims to sanctity of Luther, Bunyan and Booth seriously pressed by their admirers. It may well be that the official decision of the Roman Church or the tenacious tradition of other bodies of believers attributes sanctity to particular individuals rather than to others for misleading reasons, just as medals in wartime seldom go to all the best and bravest soldiers but to representatives selected on a somewhat arbitrary basis. It may well be also that men and women whose flaws are still apparent after conversion teach us more about Christianity than those whose sanctity has been deemed by human authority to outweigh their faults.

These converts are different and inspire others differently from those who have grown up steadily in the faith or have been converted by others. It is pointless to ask if they are better than their fellows, but certain that without them a fundamental part of the Christian message would be missing. That message for some two thousand years has been that Christ came to save sinners, not just the members of his various churches striving as best they can to live out his precepts, but also, and especially, those outside who are indifferent and even hostile. All these men and women were converted by love to love. They did not choose, they were chosen. No one will ever know just how Jesus was called to end the hidden years at Nazareth and commence his ministry, but all know why. We should not ask why each of these converts was called, but it is richly instructive to consider how they were called and how they responded.

Notes

1 The Models: Paul, Augustine and Francis

The vast literature on St Paul does not permit even of a select bibliography, but a stimulating and easily accessible introduction is Lucas Grollenberg, *Paul*, SCM Press 1978.

On St Augustine the indispensable book is Peter Brown, *Augustine of Hippo*, Faber 1967. The *Confessions* are essential reading and exist in several translations.

The sources for St Francis' life have been endlessly worked over. A convenient summary is to be found in J. Moorman, *A History of the Franciscan Order*, Oxford University Press 1968. A deliberately controversial and unconventional approach is that of A. Mockler, *Francis of Assisi, The Wandering Years*, Phaidon 1976, very useful for background information but open to serious questioning for its conclusions.

1. P. Courcelle, *Recherches sur les Confessions de St-Augustin*, Boccard 1968, p. 250 (my translation).
2. See especially Courcelle, op. cit.
3. Brown, *Augustine of Hippo*, p. 177.
4. M. D. Knowles, *The Religious Orders in England*, vol. I Cambridge University Press 1950, p. 117.
5. Mockler, *Francis of Assisi*, p. 43.
6. Quoted in Moorman, *A History of the Franciscan Order*, p. 6.
7. Ibid.
8. Moorman, op. cit., p. 9.
9. Moorman, op. cit., p. 55.

2 Martin Luther

The primary source for Luther's biography is to be found in his own remarks scattered throughout his works, especially *Table Talk*, and excellently presented in E. G. Rupp and B. Drewery, *Martin Luther*, Edward Arnold 1970. The best-known modern book on Luther is still R. H. Bainton, *Here I Stand: A Life of Martin Luther*, Hodder and Stoughton 1950, but it needs to be supplemented. Recent useful books on his early years are R. H. Fife, *The Revolt of Martin Luther*, Columbia University Press 1957, E. G. Rupp, *Luther's Progress to the Diet of Worms*, SCM Press 1951, and the finally balanced biography by J. M. Todd, *Martin Luther, A Biographical Study*, Newman, Maryland 1965.

1. Rupp and Drewery, *Martin Luther*, p. 3.
2. Ibid., p. 2.
3. Ibid., pp. 5–6.
4. W. D. J. Cargill-Thompson, 'The Problems of Luther's "Tower Experience" and its Place in his Intellectual Development', in *Religious Motivation: Biographical and Sociological Problems for the Church Historian*, Blackwell 1978.
5. Rupp and Drewery, op. cit., p. 6.
6. Todd, *Martin Luther*, p. 77.
7. A. G. Dickens, *The German Nation and Martin Luther*, Edward Arnold 1974, p. 56.
8. Todd, op. cit., p. 173.
9. Rupp and Drewery, op. cit., p. 51.
10. Ibid., p. 60.
11. R. H. Fife, *The Revolt of Martin Luther*, p. 652.
12. Todd, op. cit., p. 204.
13. Rupp, *Luther's Progress . . .*, p. 106.

3 Ignatius Loyola

The basic source is Ignatius' own dictated account, excellently presented and translated as *The Autobiography of St Ignatius Loyola*, ed. John C. Olin, Harper Torchbooks 1974. A convenient and readable commentary is J. Brodrick, SJ, *St Ignatius Loyola, the Pilgrim Years*, Burns & Oates 1956. The *Spiritual Exercises* are available in several translations, notably one by Louis J. Puhl, SJ, Westminster, Maryland 1951.

1. The details of the Manresa experience are taken from *Autobiography*, ch. 3, pp. 33–40.
2. Ibid., p. 51.
3. Ibid., p. 89.
4. Brodrick, *St Ignatius . . .*, p. 357.
5. Hugo Rahner, SJ, *Ignatius the Theologian*, Geoffrey Chapman 1968, p. 218.
6. Ibid., p. 234.
7. Ibid., p. 223.

4 Blaise Pascal

The best general book is still J. Mesnard, *Pascal, His Life and Works*, Harvill 1952. See also the much briefer essay A. J. Krailsheimer, *Pascal*, Oxford University Press 1980. Quotations are from my translation of the *Pensées*, Penguin 1966, based on the French editions of L. Lafuma of 1962 and 1963. Other editions and translations have quite different numbering.

1. Pascal, *Provincial Letters*, Penguin 1967, p. 294.

5 *Armand-Jean de Rancé*

The only serious book available is A. J. Krailsheimer, *Armand-Jean de Rancé*, Oxford University Press 1974, which though only in part a biography is at least based on documentary evidence, unlike most other studies of Rancé. Most of his vast correspondence remains unpublished, but a substantial selection of letters is being prepared for publication in the not too distant future by myself with Cistercian Publications, Kalamazoo, Michigan.

1. In his *Vie de Rancé*, 1844, really an autobiography of Chateaubriand of considerable literary merit but most misleading about its ostensible subject.
2. Quotation translated from an unpublished letter.
3. Translated into English as L. Bremond, *The Thundering Abbot*, 1930.
4. Krailsheimer, op. cit., p. 332.

6 *John Bunyan*

The primary sources for this chapter are the excellent edition, with a particularly good introduction, by R. Sharrock, of John Bunyan, *Grace Abounding*, Oxford University Press 1962, and the same editor's revision of *Pilgrim's Progress*, ed. J. B. Wharey, Oxford University Press, 1960.

1. *Grace Abounding*, p. xix. All subsequent references are to the same volume.
2. p. xxv.
3. p. 3.
4. p. xxxii.
5. p. 13.
6. p. 41.
7. p. 64.
8. p. 76.
9. p. 89.
10. p. 93.
11. p. xxvii.

7 *William Booth*

A good introduction to Booth and his work is the very readable book by Richard Collier, *The General Next to God*, Collins 1965, but for the actual documents, including many remarkable letters, and thorough discussion of the main issues the indispensable source is H. Begbie, *Life of William Booth*, 2 vols, Macmillan 1920.

1. Begbie, *Life*, vol. I, p. 77. Other references are also to vol. I.
2. p. 159.
3. p. 408.
4. p. 440.
5. p. 419.

8 Charles de Foucauld

The fullest biography of Charles de Foucauld is in French, J. F. Six, *Vie de Charles de Foucauld*, du Seuil 1962. Of the several books in English, Elizabeth Hamilton, *The Desert My Dwelling-Place*, Hodder and Stoughton 1968, is a sympathetic introduction. Foucauld's complete works are still being published in France. A useful selection is available in English as *Spiritual Autobiography of Charles de Foucauld*, ed. J. F. Six, Dimension Books, Denville, New Jersey 1964. The life of the Little Brothers of Jesus, and the inspiration of their founder, is described by René Voillaume, first Prior General, in *Au Coeur des Masses*, du Cerf 1953, translated and abridged as *Seeds of the Desert*, a new version of which appeared in 1972 from Anthony Clarke Books, Wheathampstead, Herts.

1. Six, *Vie*, p. 42.
2. Ibid., p. 237.

9 Edith Stein

The standard biography is Hilda Graef, *The Scholar and the Cross*, Longmans 1955. Additional details are to be found in C. de Miribel, *Edith Stein*, du Seuil 1954 (in French). Her collected works have been published in German, and a selection in English also exists, but they add little biographical materials.

1. In the *Oxford Dictionary of the Christian Church*, Oxford University Press[1] 1957.
2. Graef, *The Scholar and the Cross*, p. 21. All the following references are to the same work.
3. p. 32
4. p. 120.
5. p. 38.
6. p. 39.
7. p. 44
8. p. 74.
9. p. 98.
10. p. 128.
11. p. 112.
12. p. 119
13. p. 142.

10 Simone Weil

The standard biography is Simone Pétrement, *Simone Weil*, Mowbrays 1977. A very important record is J.M.Perrin and G.Thibon, *Simone Weil telle que nous l'avons connue*, Fayard 1967 (revised edition), translated as *Simone Weil as We Knew Her*, Routledge 1953, and the original text of the letter to Joë Bousquet recounting her conversion experience is in Simone Weil, *Pensées sans ordre concernant l'amour de Dieu*, 1962. Selections from her work have been published in English as *Waiting on God*, Routledge 1951, and *Gravity and Grace*, Routledge 1952. Her thoughts, mostly in fragmentary form, are preserved in her *Cahiers* (1953 and enlarged edition 1970) translated into English also twice as *Notebooks* (1956 and 1976).

1. Pétrement, *Simone Weil*, p. 215.
2. Ibid., p. 249. Both quotations are from the letter to Perrin.
3. Ibid., p. 340.
4. Ibid., p. 341.
5. Ibid., p. 526.
6. M.-M.Davy, *Simone Weil, sa Vie, son Œuvre*, Presses Universitaires de France 1966 (revised edition), p. 2 (my translation).
7. F. de Hautefeuille, *Le Tourment de Simone Weil*, Desclée de Brouwer 1970, p. 29 and p. 39 (my translation).
8. Perrin and Thibon, *Simone Weil telle que . . .*, p. 48 (my translation).
9. Ibid., p. 98.
10. Ibid., p. 111.
11. de Hautefeuille, op. cit., p. 99.
12. Ibid., p. 53.
13. Perrin and Thibon, op. cit., p. 136.
14. *Pensées sans ordre . . .*, p. 42 and 44.
15. Ibid., p. 129.
16. Perrin and Thibon, op. cit., p. 157.
17. *Cahiers II*, p. 300 (1972 ed.).

11 Thomas Merton

The Seven Storey Mountain takes Merton's autobiography up to 1943. An Epilogue describes his inner feelings up to some months following his taking of solemn vows in 1947. First published in the USA by Harcourt, Brace 1948, it did not appear unabridged in Great Britain until 1975, from Sheldon Press. Quotations are from that edition. Not all Merton's numerous other works are currently on sale, but most will be found in libraries. *The Asian Journal*, Sheldon Press 1974, is necessary reading. Until the official biography comes out, probably in 1982, a useful impression emerges from *Thomas Merton, Monk*, ed. P. Hart, Hodder and Stoughton 1974.

1. *Thomas Merton, Monk*, p. 162.
2. *Seven Storey Mountain*, p. 85.
3. Ibid., p. 184.
4. Ibid., p. 204.
5. Ibid., p. 231.
6. Ibid., p. 295.
7. Ibid., p. 318.
8. Ibid., p. 328.
9. Ibid., p. 374.
10. Ibid., p. 410.
11. *Asian Journal*, p. 116.
12. Ibid., p. 149.

13. Ibid., pp. 103–4.
14. John Eudes Bamberger, in *Thomas Merton, Monk*, pp. 37–57.
15. *Contemplation in a World of Action*, Allen & Unwin 1971, p. 186.
16. *No Man Is an Island*, Search Press 1955, pp. 116 and 120.
17. *Zen and the Birds of Appetite*, New Directions, N.Y. 1968, p. 8.
18. *Asian Journal*, p. 82.